Vivian Vande Velde

Author of Fantasy Fiction

Candie Moonshower

Enslow Publishers, Inc.
40 Industrial Road
Box 398
Berkeley Heights, NJ 07922
USA

http://www.enslow.com

My most sincere gratitude to Vivian Vande Velde—you're a lovely lady and a wonderful writer, and I've enjoyed our time together working on this book.

Special thanks to Jim and Elizabeth Vande Velde, Jane Yolen, Mary Jane Auch, and Bruce Coville for the time they spent talking to me about Vivian—you made my job easy!

Library of Congress Cataloging-in-Publication Data

Moonshower, Candie.
  Vivian Vande Velde: author of fantasy fiction / Candie Moonshower.
    p. cm.—(Authors teens love)
  Includes bibliographical references and index.
  Summary: "A biography of American author Vivian Vande Velde"—
Provided by publisher.
  ISBN-13: 978-0-7660-2964-4
  ISBN-10: 0-7660-2964-6
  1. Vande Velde, Vivian—Juvenile literature. 2. Authors, American—
20th century—Biography—Juvenile literature. 3. Young adult fiction—
Authorship—Juvenile literature. I. Title.
  PS3622.A587Z79 2009
  813'.54—dc22
  [B]
                                          2008013875
Printed in the United States of America

10 9 8 7 6 5 4 3 2 1

To Our Readers: We have done our best to make sure all Internet addresses in this book were active and appropriate when we went to press. However, the author and publisher have no control over and assume no liability for the material available on those Internet sites or on other Web sites they may link to. Any comments or suggestions can be sent by e-mail to comments@enslow.com or to the address on the back cover.

♻ Enslow Publishers, Inc., is committed to printing our books on recycled paper. The paper in every book contains 10% to 30% post-consumer waste (PCW). The cover board on the outside of each book contains 100% PCW. Our goal is to do our part to help young people and the environment too!

Photos and Illustrations: All photos courtesy of Vivian Vande Velde.

Cover Illustration: Debra Rohlfs (background illustration); portrait photo courtesy of Vivian Vande Velde (inset).

Contents

Chapter 1

Divine Intervention

When Vivian Brucato Vande Velde was a little girl in the 1950s, there were times when she wanted to be a doctor, a ballerina, a teacher, and even an astronaut. But while her ambitions were big, most did not last for longer than a day.[1] There was one dream that never left her, however. That dream was to become a writer.

Other little girls of her day grew up believing they might have careers as teachers or nurses before they married and had children. Vivian Brucato grew up in a typical American household of the times. Her mother was a homemaker. Her father earned the money. Yet, in the Brucato household, aspiring to be a writer—an unusual ambition for a young girl—was an acceptable idea and a possible career choice.

Vivian Vande Velde's dream of becoming a writer came true. Here she is at the Rochester Children's Book Festival. Vande Velde was one of the original organizers of this event.

No one ever suggested she become a writer, but the idea was always there for Vivian. "I don't remember any real epiphany I ever had about writing," Vivian says. "I do remember wanting to write, though, as a child, as far back as my memories go."[2]

It was no big secret around the neighborhood that young Vivian wanted to write. Even in elementary school, Vivian's friends knew that Vivian wanted to be a writer. "I remember once—I think between fourth or fifth grade—when I walked around all summer with a notebook," she recalls. "I was ready to write down any great ideas that came to me." Vivian says she never actually wrote any great ideas down—or any other ideas—but she was ready. "My friends, being my friends," she says, "humored me."[3]

Vivian's parents were active in her future success from the beginning. "They did a great job of convincing me I could do whatever I set my mind to," she says.[4] But writers, especially new writers, need confirmation that they are on the right track. Knowing your parents love what you do is good. But proof that comes from outside the family circle is important. Writers need an appreciative audience. Vivian got hers in the eighth grade.

All through her early school years, Vivian noticed that teachers always seemed to choose the same students' work to read aloud in class. Certain students had their papers or stories read aloud every time. But Vivian was not one of the chosen ones.

"In a classroom situation, there are always some kids who are considered to be the really good writers. They are the ones who pretty generally get their work read out loud as good examples, year after year, by teacher after teacher," Vivian recalls. "I was never one of those. I was one of the ones who might get her paper read after those—if there was time."[5]

> ## "There are always some kids who are considered to be the really good writers . . . . I was never one of those."

That changed in eighth grade at Our Lady of Good Counsel School. Vivian's teacher at the coeducational parochial school, Sister Rose Bernard, was supportive of everything that Vivian wrote. "She was the first teacher I had ever had, until that point, that was visibly enthusiastic about my writing," Vivian recalls. "Our personalities clicked. She understood my humor—and not everyone finds eighth grade girls amusing."[6]

Not only did Sister Rose Bernard read Vivian's work out loud, but the other students responded favorably, too. Vivian remembers that they laughed in all the right places. In Sister Rose Bernard's class, regular support was the norm.

This turn of events validated and sustained Vivian during an otherwise awkward time in her life. She was blossoming into a young woman, and her rapidly changing body was evidence of leaving childhood behind and approaching womanhood.

Along with the usual stresses that many young people experience during the middle school years, Vivian had an added burden. Her father had been diagnosed with lung cancer. Things were changing at home, too.

Vivian had always enjoyed constant support from her parents for her writing efforts. Now she had the compassion and attention she received from Sister Rose Bernard to help navigate this difficult time. "Sister Rose Bernard was always kind, but she had expectations that I would work hard and do my best," Vivian says.[7]

Vivian did work hard, channeling her worries into Sister Rose Bernard's assignments. "I certainly did not want to betray that trust with slipshod work," she says.[8]

Sister Rose Bernard knew how to have fun, too. For their eighth-grade graduation ceremony, the students in Sister Rose Bernard's class undertook a writing project. The girls chose contemporary songs and changed the words around to reflect their experiences at Our Lady of Good Counsel School. Vivian had a chance to use her humor and writing skills in a public way. She enjoyed it and worked hard on that project.

"We can only be grateful that I don't have copies of what we came up with for the program," she says, "though I remember at least some of our songs were based on the musical *West Side Story*. And one was the song 'Some Enchanted Evening' from the musical *South Pacific*, because Sister Rose Bernard knew that was the favorite song of one of the priests."[9]

Sister Rose Bernard did not actively steer Vivian toward a career as a novelist. But she did provide that much-needed sustenance to the writer in Vivian—positive feedback and the encouragement to keep trying. Spending eighth grade with this nun as her teacher made the year a time of great intellectual growth for Vivian. It was a time of personal growth and increasing confidence, too. Little did Vivian realize that Sister Rose Bernard would be only the first of countless readers to enjoy her stories and "get" her humor.

Sadly, Vivian's family has lost track of Sister Rose Bernard in the years since Vivian attended Our Lady of Good Counsel School. Sister Rose Bernard has never left Vivian's heart or memory, though. Vivian had the good nun in mind later in life when she wrote her novel *Smart Dog*. In the book, the character of Sister Mary Grace teaches fifth grade and not eighth, as Sister Rose Bernard did. But, just as in real life, Sister Mary Grace is as fun and supportive a teacher as Sister Rose Bernard.

There are many scenes in *Smart Dog* that surely depict the kindness and good humor Vivian remembered about her time with Sister Rose Bernard. One such scene is when Sister Mary Grace discovers the dog, F-32, which has come to school with Amy Prochenko:

At least, Amy thought, *Sister Mary Grace seems more puzzled than angry*. In fact—Amy started breathing again—Sister Mary Grace began to laugh. She liked to say that she had been a teacher for almost forty years, and there wasn't much she hadn't seen or heard before. Now she tapped on the glass and pretended to scold. "Dogs go to dog school; people go to people school."[10]

Vivian Brucato Vande Velde has published over thirty books. She has received countless awards for her work. Young people everywhere enjoy reading her stories. Sister Rose Bernard would be proud—but surely not surprised.

Chapter 2

Clickety-Clack

"I was born on the same day as Beatle Paul McCartney, but I'm not as old as him," Vivian Brucato Vande Velde shares.[1] Vivian Brucato was born on June 18, 1951, in New York City. Vivian would grow up to write stories. Paul McCartney was well on his way to becoming one-half of the writing team, Lennon and McCartney (with his bandmate, John Lennon). Along with their friends, George Harrison and Ringo Starr, they would form one of the best-known rock-and-roll bands of all time, the Beatles. The Beatles shaped the music of a generation—Vivian's generation—during Vivian's teen years.

But before Vivian reached her teens and the United States launched into a tumultuous and chaotic time in its history, the future writer

Marcelle and Pat Brucato.

Vivian in 1951 with her brother, Allan

enjoyed a peaceful childhood. The nation had come through World War II and the Korean War. Even against the backdrop of the Cold War—a time of tension and ideological conflict between the United States and the Soviet Union—Americans were enjoying a time of unprecedented prosperity. Compared to the war years that came before and a whirlwind of changes that were on the way in the 1960s, the mid-1950s felt like a calm time focused on family and country.

Vivian's mother, Marcelle, was born in Italy and raised in France as a French citizen. Vivian's father, Pasquale Brucato—called "Pat"—was a soldier in the U.S. Army during World War II. Pat met Marcelle in Nice, France, where she taught French at a Berlitz Language School. Many American G.I.s met and married their "war brides" while serving in Europe. Pat Brucato followed this path. Pat and Marcelle married in 1946 in Nice, France.

After the war, the Brucatos came back to the United States and settled in Pat's home town—New York City. Their first child, a son named Allan, was born in 1950. Vivian came along in 1951.

Pat spoke French, too. "My father was an American and spoke English, too, of course," Vivian recalls, "but he sounded like a Hungarian!"[2] After Allan and Vivian were born, Pat and Marcelle continued to speak French in the home to their children. French was Allan and Vivian's first language. Speaking English came later.

15

While they lived in New York City, Marcelle continued to work as a language teacher at the Berlitz Language School there, teaching French and Italian. The family moved soon after Vivian was born, first to Medina, New York, and then to Rochester, New York, when Vivian was two years old. In Rochester, Marcelle became a stay-at-home mom.

Pat got a job working at the daily newspaper, the *Rochester Democrat & Chronicle*. He worked nights as a linotype operator. Pat was not writing the news stories that appeared in the paper, but as a linotype operator, he was in charge of casting lines of type, which, when inked, would produce newsprint.

Pat might not have wanted to be a journalist, but he was interested in writing. Since he worked at night, he spent part of his days writing. Seeing someone in her own household working at writing was powerful. It reinforced the idea that writing was a worthy profession to pursue.

Pat had, over the years, began writing fiction, receiving some rejections for his work. Sometimes, at his job with the newspaper, Pat and his friends wrote bogus news stories and ran them off as jokes![3]

But Pat's passion, as far back as Vivian could remember, was for writing radio plays.[4] Before the television set became a common household appliance, most people listened to the radio. Radio programs provided people with their news and

The Brucato family in 1953.

their entertainment. Radio plays, or radio dramas, were wildly popular until the mid-1950s.

Vivian's father had an old typewriter that he used for his writing. "You had to pound the keys with great force to get it to work," Vivian recalls. "I don't remember a time that I didn't hear the clacking of those keys."[5]

Pat's pounding at the typewriter was the background noise in Vivian's life. Hearing and seeing her father working at the typewriter was significant. It reinforced for Vivian the idea that one could aspire to be a writer—that writing was an acceptable occupation.

The Brucatos did not have a large extended family. Marcelle's parents lived overseas. Pat's father lived in New York City and visited at times, but he passed away when Vivian was five years old. Even without a lot of relatives, the Brucatos— Pat, Marcelle, Allan, and Vivian—were a very happy family.

Reading came easily to Vivian. Vivian remembers that her father, Pat, spent a lot of time reading to the children at home. She feels this contributed to her early love of reading—and her aptitude at reading, too.

She remembers her father reading L. Frank Baum's *The Wizard of Oz* to her and her older brother, Allan. *The Wizard of Oz* was not the first book he read to his children, but it is the first one Vivian recalls. *The Wizard of Oz* contains elements of fantasy, wizardry, and witchcraft. The fact that

The Wizard of Oz is the first book she remembers was significant when Vivian began to write novels.

When Allan entered kindergarten, the Brucatos realized that he needed to speak English in school, so the family worked to immerse their children in English. "Once we knew English," Vivian recalls, "we reverted to French at home for a while."[6]

Vivian was quite skillful at reading by the time she entered kindergarten. Her brother, Allan, was in first grade. "I was reading along with Allan," she says, "and so I went to school knowing a bit more than I would have otherwise."[7]

Vivian's family pets were dogs. After their first dog, Belle (which is French for beautiful), passed on, Ringle came to live with the family. Ringle was a German shepherd mix, with white and gray coloring—a striking, good-looking dog, as Vivian remembers him. The name, Ringle, came from the sound that Vivian thought a bell makes.[8]

Vivian's parents taught Ringle to respond to commands in French, while Allan and Vivian taught Ringle to respond to commands in English. Vivian was convinced that Ringle was a superintelligent dog.

Whenever Vivian had problems or felt sad, Ringle would gaze at Vivian with her big brown eyes. Vivian believed that Ringle could understand everything she told the dog. "I had the impression that Ringle was more beautiful than we were. I felt like the plain baby swan compared to the cute ducklings in the story of "The Ugly Duckling"— even compared to my dog," Vivian recalls. "And I

Vivian and Allan in 1953 with Ringle, the inspiration for *Smart Dog*.

knew, even then, that some ugly ducklings remain ugly ducklings, which struck me as unfair."[9]

Vivian asked herself, "What if Ringle could act and talk?"[10] Those musings later became the genesis for her book, *Smart Dog*. In *Smart Dog*, fifth grader Amy Prochenko meets a dog that speaks to her—in English! F-32 is a dog that has run away from the college lab where he lives—and where scientists have been using him for research into canine intelligence. F-32 is "a medium-sized dog with floppy ears and big brown eyes and long fur that was equal parts brown and white and black."[11] F-32 is, indeed, a dog that looks and acts just as Vivian's dog Ringle did.

From her earliest memories, Vivian wanted to write. She taught herself to type, but she could never type quickly enough to keep up with the stories in her mind. It worked better for Vivian to handwrite her stories. Then, she recalls, she could go back and change her mind—even mid-word.[12]

As a youngster, Vivian was always making up stories. Sometimes, she and Allan played games that involved stories they made up together.

"We had a collaboration of sorts," she says with a laugh. "I might have Barbie dressing up and going to a dance, and Allan would have Godzilla eating Barbie. And our parents always said, 'It's good!' No matter what we showed them, they gave us their approval."[13]

In school, Vivian found that like so many kids, she was not a student that teachers always noticed. "Teachers would read out loud, and certain students' papers were always read out loud—every time!" Vivian recalls. "I wasn't one of 'the chosen' at all."[14] That did not stop Vivian from writing her stories, though.

When Vivian reached eighth grade at Our Lady of Good Counsel School, her situation changed. This is when Sister Rose Bernard took an interest in Vivian. Vivian describes the experience as a "click" between her and the nun.[15] Sister Rose Bernard understood the humor in what Vivian was writing and began to read her stories out loud to the class.

Eighth grade was a turbulent time in the world, and in Vivian's life—her father remained ill with cancer. Vivian continued to be an avid reader. She remembers "studying the dead white guys,"[16] the traditional canon for English studies. During this time, aided by her brother, Allan, Vivian's world exploded on an intellectual level. Allan, a freshman in high school, brought home his ninth-grade reading assignments. Vivian began reading Allan's books, as well as her own.

"It was a time of great intellectual exploration and growth for me," she says. "These were more grown-up books."[17] Some of the books she read included *The Fellowship of the Ring* by J.R.R. Tolkien, *The Once and Future King* by T.H. White, and *The Catcher in the Rye* by J.D. Salinger. "I was reading these books and thinking, 'Wow!'" she says.[18]

T.H. White's *The Once and Future King* solidified for Vivian what kinds of stories she wanted to write. "It's the story of King Arthur—not a scholarly search for the Dark Ages, historic Arthur, but a story full of anachronisms and peopled by interesting, flawed characters," Vivian says. "I couldn't tell who to root for because they were often on opposing sides—yet I cared deeply for all of them."[19]

"I always knew I wanted to be an author, but it was when I was in eighth grade and read T.H. White's *The Once and Future King* that I absolutely knew what kind of story I wanted to write," Vivian says.[20] Vivian's future novels would be peopled by fairy-tale heroes and heroines brought to life to look and act like real kids—seemingly normal, but flawed and interesting.

In those days, the early 1960s, there were not as many books available that had been written specifically for young adults. "I went pretty much from children's books to adult books," Vivian says.[21]

Vivian's parents were members of the *Reader's Digest* Condensed Books Club, and Vivian read many of those books, too. "Now I'm horrified at the idea of abridged versions, but in my own defense, I think I started reading them when I was too young to know what the word 'condensed' meant," she says.[22] Those condensed versions of current best sellers and classic books did give Vivian a broad range of reading choices.

That same year, Vivian read *To Kill a Mockingbird* by Harper Lee. The first time she read it was in the *Reader's Digest* condensed version.

(Later, of course, she read the book in its original published form.)[23] Vivian thought the book was incredible. She had no idea at the time that it had won several major awards for literature. She did not even know, until several years later, that *To Kill a Mockingbird* was one of the most beloved books of her time.[24] Lee's characters, so real to life and capable of eliciting deep emotions, influenced Vivian, too. It still remains her favorite book. "When I am absolutely pinned down to name one book as being the best in American literature," she says, "that's it."[25]

Vivian liked to read late into the night, and her habit of reading late often got her in trouble with her parents. "At night my parents would tell me, 'Finish that chapter, then lights out.' But I'd get so caught up in the story that (sometimes unintentionally, sometimes without even noticing), I often just kept on reading."[26]

Eighth grade was a time of rapid physical growth as well. Vivian was blossoming into a young woman as she finished the school year and prepared to attend an all-girls parochial high school. It was 1965. Paul McCartney and the Beatles were exploding onto the American music scene with their album *Meet the Beatles*. In the nine years that Vivian had been in school, social customs had changed, the culture had changed, and the world was changing, too. A new conflict had begun in far-off Vietnam, and that conflict would define Vivian's high-school years.

Chapter 3

All Girls

Leaving the safety of Sister Rose Bernard's eighth grade classroom and entering high school might have been a scary time for Vivian. High school is often a time of new beginnings. Friendships that have survived for years are lost when people are separated. Finding a comfortable path in a new school can be hard. Vivian's fears were lessened, however, by the fact that her high school, a Catholic school called Nazareth Academy, was an all-girls school.

Before Vivian could settle into her new high-school routine, though, she suffered a tragic loss. Her father, Pat, died of lung cancer in November of 1965. Vivian's mother, Marcelle, decided to take Vivian and Allan to France. Marcelle had only been back to her home country of France twice, both times before Vivian's birth. Marcelle had not seen her family in a number of years. At this sad time, Marcelle packed up her children and traveled to France for a lengthy visit with her family.

Vivian and Allan had spoken fluent French before they began attending school. But their French skills had diminished over the years as they were immersed in English at school. In France, the loss of their father weighed heavily on Vivian and Allan. Their grief, combined with their lack of adequate French language skills, made communicating with their French relatives difficult. Vivian and Allan felt isolated. "I'm sure we weren't the best of company," Vivian recalls.[1]

Vivian, Allan, and their mother stayed in France during November and December of Vivian's freshman year. She and Allan missed several weeks of school.[2] When the Brucatos returned to Rochester, Vivian's high-school years began in earnest. Marcelle explained their situation to their teachers. Vivian and Allan had to work hard to catch up on the learning and lessons they had missed while in France.

The faculty at Nazareth Academy stressed leadership and worked to instill in the girls the belief that women can do anything that men can do. Vivian remembers her years at Nazareth as a positive experience. "Since there were no boys around constantly watching the girls," she says, "we were not afraid to try new things."[3]

Vivian continued her habit of avid reading. She liked authors such as Edgar Allan Poe and Arthur

Conan Doyle. She enjoyed Mary Renault's stories of ancient Greece. She also read Graham Greene (though she says she did not always understand his works). John Steinbeck was a favorite author of Vivian's, too. "I have to put in a plug for his never-completed work, *The Acts of King Arthur and His Noble Knights*," she says, "which was published posthumously and probably would have been a masterpiece."[4]

Plays and drama caught Vivian's interest, and she began to read a lot of plays, although she was not able to attend many. Vivian thinks that reading so many plays may explain, as she says, "why I favor action and dialogue and have little patience with description."[5]

Vivian joined the Drama Club in high school, and she wrote for the school newspaper, *The Gabriel*, too. Writing for both the Drama Club and *The Gabriel* helped Vivian gain confidence. She was sharing her work with a broader audience than just her teachers and her closest friends. "This was my first public exposure as a writer—and no one stoned me!" Vivian recalls. "And the nuns didn't take away my writing privileges."[6]

Throughout high school, Vivian continued to write. At that point, she was not planning to make any attempts toward publication. When she was a senior, however, Vivian wrote a play. She took the legend of the fall of Troy and retold it from the point of view of the females. In the legend of the fall of Troy, Greek forces, under the leadership of King Menelaus, sail to Troy in Asia Minor.

There they wage a ten-year war to win back Helen, the famous Greek beauty who was taken away by the Trojan prince, Paris.

Vivian showed her play to her drama teacher. The drama teacher appeared to be impressed with Vivian's efforts, but she did not offer to present the play. Not to be deterred, Vivian went to the library and found a copy of *Writer's Market*. *Writer's Market* is a large book, published annually, that lists the majority of book and magazine publishers and their submission guidelines for writing. Vivian chose several publishing houses she thought might be appropriate places to submit her play, and sent it out.

> ## "I began to figure that it was not as good a play as I'd believed it might be."

Vivian's play was rejected a number of times. "I was disappointed, but not devastated," Vivian says. "I began to figure that it was not as good a play as I'd believed it might be."[7] After five or so rejections, Vivian gave up on submitting the play and retired it to a drawer.

Vivian's years in high school, 1965 through 1969, were a turbulent time in the history of the United States. The Vietnam War was in full swing. People throughout the country were conflicted about the social, cultural, and philosophical issues of the times. From the safe and benign post-World War II years of the 1950s—Vivian's childhood years—the country had launched into a chaotic and unstable time of changing attitudes, changing behaviors, and changing clothing.

Vivian recalls feeling somewhat ambivalent about the Vietnam War—a sense of being of two minds about the conflict in far-off Asia. "I didn't want to be involved," she says, "and I was torn both ways."[8] Vivian was not an active antiwar protestor, as many high school and college students were at that time, but she did feel conflicted.

Vivian often wondered how her father, Pat, a veteran of World War II, would have felt about the Vietnam War. This is not surprising. Attitudes about the validity of the United States' participation in the two wars were completely polarized. The veterans of World War II, a war that had the complete support of the population of the United States, were regarded as heroes upon their return stateside. Now, with Vietnam, there was an overall negative perception of the war. Soldiers returning from Vietnam, through no fault of their own, often found themselves reviled and mistreated.

Even at an all-girls parochial school, Vivian and her fellow students were not isolated. She remembers the teachers actively working to prepare the girls for college. The students talked about world events. "The nuns realized that we girls needed to be familiar with what was happening in our own backyards—and the world, too," Vivian says.[9] Classroom discussions were vigorous and wide reaching in content.

Not all of high school was serious business, however. Even in times of cultural upheaval, teenagers will find ways to have fun. Vivian and her friends were no exception. The 1960s were an exciting time intellectually, culturally, and socially. One aspect of the 1960s made Vivian glad she was attending parochial school, though—the changing fashion styles. Vivian did not mind wearing the parochial school uniform as much as some of her friends. "I thought that the clothes in the 1960s were terrible," she says with a laugh.[10] Wearing a uniform to school each day alleviated a lot of style problems for Vivian.

Dating is a rite of passage in high school, too. Vivian recalls being at a distinct disadvantage in the realm of dating. Since she attended an all-girls school, it was hard to get to know boys outside of school. Vivian was dependent on her friends' brothers and her brother's friends as dating prospects. It was a lot of trouble, she found! This lessened her interest in dating during her high-school years.[11]

Later in life, Vivian would write *A Well-Timed Enchantment*, a book that she acknowledges as autobiographical in many respects. "I'm certain that I had our time in France, after the death of my father, in mind when I wrote *A Well-Timed Enchantment*," Vivian says.[12] The opening of the

Vivian with her beloved father, Pat, and her mother and brother. Pat Brucato died just as Vivian entered high school, and Marcelle took her and Allan to France, a trip that is mirrored later in her book, *A Well-Timed Enchantment*.

book introduces Deanna, whose parents are divorced. Her mother has taken Deanna to visit relatives in France. Deanna does not know her relatives, and getting to know them is a task hampered by Deanna's complete inability to speak French. This scene closely mirrors Vivian's own experience in France after the death of her father:

> These French people were her maternal relatives: aunts, uncles and cousins her mother hadn't seen in years, people Deanna had never seen. They'd give her big kisses, one on each cheek, and smile at her. *"Ne parle t-elle pas français?"* they'd ask, which Deanna learned meant "Doesn't she speak French?" And her mother would rattle off an explanation of how Deanna had spoken a little when she'd been very young but had forgotten it all.[13]

In *A Well-Timed Enchantment*, Deanna makes friends with a cat, Oliver. When she loses her Mickey Mouse watch in a well, she is transported into the past, in France, "just north of 1066."[14] Oliver shows up there as a mysterious (and cute) sidekick. Their strange and fantastical journey into the past teaches her that things—and, especially, people—are not always as they seem. This is a theme that will show up in all of Vivian's future works.

High school was a happy, productive time for Vivian. It was also a time during which, unwittingly perhaps, she was preparing for her future. Writing for the Drama Club and the school news-paper, gave Vivian an opportunity to expand her readership. And the experience of having her play rejected was also a positive experience, teaching Vivian that, as her father Pat had experienced, a writer's life is not always easy.

Although it was not always easy, the writer's life certainly would provide Vivian with much emotional satisfaction in the near future. Remembering her nights of getting into trouble with her parents for reading late, Vivian admits that this is what she wanted to do in the future: "Write stories that were so engrossing I would get other kids in trouble with their parents."[15]

High school got off to a rocky start with the death of Vivian's beloved father, Pat. It ended on a calm note, however, even as the world outside of Nazareth Academy was in turmoil. Vivian graduated in 1969. College awaited her in the fall.

Chapter 4

Speed Typing—But Not Writing

After graduating from Nazareth Academy in Rochester, Vivian went off to college at State University of New York, called SUNY, in Brockport, New York. She began her freshman year there in the fall of 1969.

President Richard Nixon was in his first term in office. (Nixon would later become the first president to resign from office.) The United States had been officially involved in the Vietnam War for four years. Women were liberating themselves and choosing alternative lifestyles from those of their mothers before them. Instead of marrying young and starting families right away, many young women, like Vivian, were going off to college to pursue higher education.

It was an interesting era in which to begin college. College campuses across the United States were experiencing upheaval brought on by the conflict in Vietnam. Many students were foregoing typical business and job-oriented courses of study to pursue degrees in philosophy, literature, history, and political science.

Although Vivian never engaged in antiwar demonstrations, she noticed that many students spent their college years to protesting the war. Some students spent their time in college "tuning out and turning on"—a euphemism of the times that referred to ignoring many of the traditions of their parents and, in some cases, engaging in drug use. On some college campuses, professors joined their students in protesting the war.

Young men old enough to be drafted into the war—and who could not afford to attend college—were inducted into the military and sent overseas. Some came home alive. Many did not. And, sadly, a few students lost their lives right here in the United States in antiwar protests, such as that which took place on the campus of Kent State University in May of 1970, when four students died.

Vivian, a literary-minded freshman, had no interest in studying math, science, philosophy, or foreign languages. She wanted to read great literature. She ignored all the usual prerequisites of the typical underclassman and concentrated on literature. Vivian took all of the literature classes she could in that one year, declaring herself an English major with a political science minor. But after one year, Vivian decided, "Well, enough. I've taken all of the courses I'm interested in taking."[1]

Vivian dropped out of the State University of New York and returned home to Rochester in 1970. She enrolled in the Rochester Business Institute, signing up for an eighteen-month-long program of classes that would teach her speed typing, shorthand, and business accounting. These courses, Vivian knew, would prepare her for work as a secretary.[2]

Even though opportunities for women were beginning to open up in the late 1960s, it was still a man's world as far as career choices. Women made up the majority of the work force in areas such as teaching and working in offices as secretaries or typists. Nineteen-year-old Vivian figured that a secretarial course was a practical plan of action likely to land her a job.

During her time at the Rochester Business Institute, Vivian did not work at her creative writing. Since the play she had written as a senior in high school, she had not written any more plays or stories. Vivian was not writing any fiction at all. Her writing consisted of her school assignments now. These assignments were extremely useful in nature as befitted the sensible, job-oriented certification Vivian was pursuing.

After graduating from her secretarial training at the Rochester Business Institute, Vivian found a position as a secretary at the Rochester Telephone Company. She still lived with her mother. The

Vivian Brucato in 1972.

work she did each day was not very exciting for young Vivian. She enjoyed the people at the telephone company, but it was simply a job. She knew that there had to be something else out there for her, but Vivian was not sure yet what the future might hold.[3]

In 1973, Vivian had worked at the Rochester Telephone Company for two years. She was not dating anyone special. A friend, Sylviane, invited Vivian to a cookout at one of her friend's homes. There, she introduced Vivian to a young man. "At first," Vivian recalls, "I thought my friend was trying to get rid of one of her old boyfriends. I met Jim, and I wondered why she would want to dump him. He was so nice, and warm and funny, too!"[4]

Jim was grilling steaks, and Sylviane and Vivian were making a mess of his kitchen trying to cook brownies. It was, Vivian remembers, the start of a beautiful relationship.[5]

Jim Vande Velde worked with computers at the Kodak Company in Rochester. He was a middle manager there during the early days of computers. Jim was twenty-six years old when he met Vivian. In the beginning of their friendship, Jim had no idea Vivian had any aspirations to write. "I just knew she was a wonderful, bright, energetic, caring and beautiful person," he says.[6]

Vivian and Jim were married on April 20, 1974. The couple happily embarked upon their married life. They enjoyed spending time together. They spent a lot of time talking, reading, and bicycling together. In 1975, Vivian and Jim

In 1974, Vivian Brucato married Jim Vande Velde. From left to right: Allan, Marcelle, Vivian, Jim, and Jim's parents, Virginia and Chuck.

purchased a house. They spent their hours outside of their jobs working on their first home. Vivian continued working as a secretary at the Rochester Telephone Company for several years, while Jim pursued his career at Kodak.

The young couple settled into their new home and began to consolidate their belongings. They discovered that they owned many of the same books and albums. "Jim is a big reader, too, so we talked quite a bit about the books we both enjoyed," Vivian says. "At that point, I began to talk to Jim about my desire to write a book."[7]

On April 2, 1979, the Vande Velde family grew when Vivian and Jim's daughter, Elizabeth, was born. Vivian quit her job at the telephone company to stay at home and raise Elizabeth. The family lived in the town of Greece, a suburb of Rochester.

Vivian recalls that it was Jim who first noticed that she needed some kind of activity that would get her outside the house. When he came home from work during that first year of Elizabeth's life, the baby would be crying and Vivian would feel quite frazzled. Although Jim did not have any idea when he met Vivian that she was at all interested in writing, he wasted no time when he did find out.[8] Jim discovered, through the Greece Continuing Education Department, that a course was available. That course was called "Writing for Publication."

Jim encouraged Vivian to sign up for the course. It took place at night, so Vivian could leave Elizabeth in Jim's capable hands and leave without

Daughter Elizabeth's baptism in 1979. From left to right: Jim, Vivian (holding Elizabeth), and Elizabeth's godmother, Marianne Beatson.

worrying. For one night a week, Vivian could get out of the house for a few hours. "It was quite a surprise to find out what a great writer Vivian was to become," Jim says.[9]

The course lasted ten weeks. When it was over, Vivian signed up for the course again. "I took that course a couple of times," she says. "It was the same course, but it was a much-needed night out and a break for me."[10] Jim was supportive. "I encouraged Vivian because this was something she wanted to pursue," Jim says.[11]

That course, "Writing for Publication," reignited Vivian's interest in writing. Her years of speed typing over, Vivian now began to write again, in earnest.

Vivian and Jim's daughter, Elizabeth, has many memories of those early years in her mother's writing career. "One of my earliest memories is of my mom being at her Apple II computer (with the green type on the screen). Sometimes she'd be typing away late into the night, or sometimes she'd get up in the middle of the night to get an idea down on paper," Elizabeth says.[12]

It would not be long before Vivian's ideas were transformed into stories—and a novel for teenagers.

Chapter 5

A Major Project of My Own

During her "Writing for Publication" course, Vande Velde's one night a week out of the house quickly transformed from a night to escape to a night to write. Vande Velde's lifelong interest in writing fiction came to life again.

Vande Velde's teacher assigned many writing exercises in the beginning weeks of her first go-round in the class. All of the exercises seemed oriented toward writing mysteries for adults. Vande Velde did not pay too much attention to classifying her writing as any particular genre. She wrote steadily, never taking the time to decide whether her stories were "for adults" or "for children." She was enjoying her creative time and not putting too much pressure on herself.[1]

Vande Velde's teacher made two memorable

Jim, Vivian, and Elizabeth Vande Velde. At this time, Vivian Vande Velde was studying "Writing for Publication" through the Greece Continuing Education Department.

comments during the course. For Vande Velde, both comments would prove to be life changing with regard to her writing.[2] The first comment occurred one night when, during a read-aloud time, the teacher said to the class, "Let's see who Viv has polished off in her story this week." The teacher was referring to Vande Velde's tendency to kill off her characters.[3]

That comment prompted Vande Velde to change her focus. She admits that her change in focus was, at the time, a knee-jerk reaction. "I decided, then and there, that I would make my work-in-progress a sweet children's story," Vande Velde says.[4]

Vande Velde had always enjoyed fairy tales and fantasy, from the time she remembered her father reading the magical *Wizard of Oz* stories to her. She was bothered, though, by the way the main characters in fairy tales always turned out to be self-assured princesses. "These princesses were always quite smart, and resourceful, too," she says, "and they could sing, too, of course!"[5]

Vande Velde wanted to write a story in which the main character would not be gorgeous and self-assured. She wanted a character who knows she is not pretty—even when her father insists that she is beautiful. "I wanted a princess who was exactly *not* like the beautiful, self-confident princesses in the Disney movies," Vande Velde says.[6]

Vande Velde's main character would meet a handsome prince, yes, as the beautiful princesses always do in fairy tales. But Vande Velde's storied handsome prince would be stubborn and not very bright. Vande Velde's main character—the smart, resourceful but not pretty princess—would have to rescue the prince, she decided.[7]

In short, Vande Velde wanted a main character that was more like her.

Vande Velde gave a lot of thought to her princess as she continued to hone her writing skills. She was less frazzled at home because she had something on her mind—a renewed interest in writing that delighted her. She found it enjoyable to talk to adults one night a week. Even more fun was that she was spending time with a group of people who were all writing stories. And all her classmates were approaching their stories from different directions.

The second pivotal comment that Vande Velde's teacher made was seemingly offhand. "I'm assuming that you are all working on major projects of your own," Vande Velde's teacher said one night as she handed out various assignments.[8]

Vande Velde recalls thinking, "Oh yeah! I'd better get on that!" And that night, she started writing what was to become *A Hidden Magic*.[9]

During this exciting time in Vande Velde's life, she had two major, important projects—being a full-time mom to baby Elizabeth and the writing of *A Hidden Magic*. Mothering was pleasurable and ongoing. But writing? Not so much! Vande Velde remembers that she frequently set aside her work on the novel to pursue other creative projects, like knitting and crocheting. "I wanted to work on projects where you see tangible progress," she says. "With writing, it is hard to see any measurable progress."[10]

Vande Velde's husband, Jim, remembers her early years as a writer as ones of complete dedication on Vande Velde's part. "She worked very hard to get the manuscripts just perfect," he says.[11] Vande Velde laughingly recalls that she allowed herself to get distracted many times. But each time she picked up the novel and began to work on it again, Vande Velde found the characters calling out to her. Over the course of the next two years, Vande Velde finished her first novel, *A Hidden Magic*.

"*A Hidden Magic* started with the character," Vande Velde says. "Princess Jennifer has hair that misbehaves (I have to admit that wild hair is a recurring theme in quite a few of my stories). She is quite shy, doesn't want to have an adventure, and she keeps on hoping that someone else will come in and solve her problems for her."[12]

Vande Velde knew that she would start the story with "Once upon a time," and that it had to end with "And they lived happily ever after."[13] In between, she would have to have some adventures happen for Jennifer so that there would be a plot. That part—writing the middle—was where the hard work came in.

In the book, Vande Velde introduces her readers to the unusual princess, Jennifer, in this way: "Now Jennifer was not your average beautiful princess living in a magnificent palace. In fact, she was actually rather plain and shy, with the chubby, good-natured kind of face parents tend to call nice."[14]

Plain, shy Jennifer does, indeed, meet a handsome prince, Alexander: "He had curly golden hair, deep blue eyes, and very broad shoulders. His suit was gleaming white satin, and he had a marvelous maroon velvet cloak with fur trim. Everywhere about him there were flashes and sparkles as the sun reflected on gold buckles and rings."[15]

With apparent good reason, the handsome prince Alexander is also very conceited, having a habit of "practicing disarming smiles."[16] In his journeys, he has offended every person he has encountered. In addition to being conceited, Alexander is not all that bright, as it turns out.

One of the people he offends is Malveenya, a witch of extraordinary powers. Malveenya puts Alexander into a deep sleep. Jennifer realizes that she is not really in love with Alexander, but she does not feel right about leaving him under the evil spell. She sets out to find a way to help him.

Jennifer meets Norman, a young sorcerer. Reminiscent of Dorothy and her friends' encounter with the Wizard of Oz in the Emerald City in L. Frank Baum's story, Jennifer encounters Norman at the doorway to his home. In the beginning, Norman is fierce and frightening, much as the Wizard is in *The Wizard of Oz*. He scares Jennifer by bellowing at her.

But Jennifer scolds Norman for frightening her—just as Dorothy scolds the Wizard for frightening the Cowardly Lion in *The Wizard of Oz*. And just as the Wizard is revealed to Dorothy as simply a man, like any other, Norman shrinks and becomes his real self. And his real self, with his frizzy red hair and kind eyes, impresses Jennifer more than Alexander's good looks ever could.

School Library Journal, a magazine for school librarians, would call *A Hidden Magic* "an original and delightful parody of the classic fairy-tale genre."[17] The novel would be named by *American Bookseller* as a "Pick of the Lists." It was also named a "Notable Children's Trade Book in the Language Arts" by the National Council of Teachers in English. All the accolades that *A Hidden Magic* received were high praises, indeed, for a first novel.

From the first book Vande Velde recalls her father reading to her—*The Wizard of Oz*—to the development of a major project of her own, Vande Velde's dream of becoming a published author was coming true. *A Hidden Magic* would be the first novel a publisher offered to buy from the budding author. Due to unexpected circumstances, however, *A Hidden Magic* would not be the first of Vande Velde's works to hit the bookshelves.

Chapter 6

A Hidden Magic

*U*nlike a lot of new novelists, Vande Velde was familiar with the way the submission process works in the writing business. Her experience of watching her father submit his radio plays to various publishers—unsuccessfully—had taught her a great deal. In high school, Vande Velde had put that knowledge to work when she explored the *Writer's Market* book for possible publishers for her play about the fall of Troy.

Now, with a novel manuscript finished, Vande Velde went to the library to explore the *Writer's Market* again. She found a number of possible publishers for *A Hidden Magic*. In fact, Vande Velde made a list of thirty-two possibilities for her new book! With some hope and excitement, Vande Velde mailed the manuscript of her novel out to thirty-two publishing houses. Then she began the nerve-wracking wait.[1]

While she waited to hear from editors at the thirty-two publishing houses about *A Hidden Magic*, Vande Velde worked on a number of short stories. She did not, however, begin a new novel. Over time, Vande Velde began to hear from editors. The news was not good. She received thirty-two rejections on *A Hidden Magic*. Every publisher Vande Velde had chosen from the *Writer's Market* had rejected it. All thirty-two of her chosen "possibilities" had to be crossed off her list.[2]

Vande Velde was not totally deflated. In the time she had been waiting to hear from the publishers about her novel, she had received acceptances for several short stories. A story entitled "Salvatore and the Leprechaun" was published in *Cricket* magazine in 1982. *Highlights* magazine accepted a story called "The Dragon, the Unicorn, and the Caterpillar," although it would not make it to print until years later.

Vande Velde had finished writing *A Hidden Magic* in 1981, when she was thirty years old and the mother of a small child. In those days, personal computers were rare, and Vande Velde typed all her manuscripts on a typewriter. Typewriters— even snazzy electric ones—did not have any type of word-processing tools on them at that time. There was no way to move, copy and paste, or even quickly edit material that needed to be changed. If a writer wanted to shift material, entire sections of a long written work had to be typed again. Any mistakes beyond simple typographical errors that could be erased and typed over necessitated the retyping of entire pages. "I would type more and more slowly as I neared the bottom of each page," Vande Velde says, "so I wouldn't make mistakes and have to start over."[3]

Sometimes, Vande Velde's manuscripts returned to her looking bedraggled. She did not want to submit a rough, creased manuscript to a new editor. Vande Velde would find that she needed to retype some or all of her stories or her novel. As she retyped her words, she would reread her stories. "At the risk of sounding egotistical," she says, "I was surprised and pleased to find that I still enjoyed the stories!"[4]

This was an important realization. Vande Velde surmised that it was not necessarily her stories that were earning the rejections. This insight led to the realization that she was sending her work to the *wrong* publishing houses.[5] Vande Velde figured out that, eventually, she was bound to find the right publisher for her work. If she persevered, she figured, a publisher was bound to say yes—the right publisher.

Many of the rejections that Vande Velde received gave her conflicting information. Some of the rejection letters suggested that since *A Hidden Magic* was a satire—a spoof, or sarcastic story— that she should send the manuscript to publishers of adult books. The houses that published books for adults suggested that since the manuscript was a fairy tale, Vande Velde should send it to companies that published stories for children.[6]

One rejection Vande Velde received really angered her. She recalls what it said: "Kids like their fantasies to be fantastic, not like you or me or the kid down the street. We're not currently accepting children's literature, but even if we were, we wouldn't take this one."[7]

Rejections like these might have defeated another writer, but not Vande Velde. With publisher number thirty-three, Vande Velde found her "right" publisher. Crown Publishers (now a part of Random House) said that magical, fantastical word that every writer wants to hear: "Yes."[8]

> ## Rejections like these might have defeated another writer, but not Vande Velde.

Vande Velde had chosen Crown Publishers for submission number thirty-three because of her rejection letters. Since so many editors seemed divided on whether *A Hidden Magic* was a satire for adults or a fairy tale for children, Vande Velde decided to send the manuscript to Crown.[9] Vande Velde owned a book published by Crown. That book, *The Unknown Web* by Richard Adams, was a collection of stories.

Vande Velde enjoyed Adams' stories, but she had never been able to decide if they had been written for children or adults. Because Crown had published *The Unknown Web* and other books for both children and adults, Vande Velde thought it made sense to send *A Hidden Magic* to Crown.

Vande Velde had finished *A Hidden Magic* in 1981. Now, during Thanksgiving week of 1983, she received the long-awaited letter. Editor Thea Feldman wrote: "I'm interested in your story, and I want to talk to you."[10] As it was a holiday weekend, Vande Velde was not able to reach Ms. Feldman for several days. Vande Velde waited, fretting and wondering, until she could contact the editor. "I hardly dared to believe that Thea Feldman's letter might lead to a contract offer," Vande Velde says.[11]

Thea Feldman's letter did, indeed, lead to a contract offer, which Vande Velde happily accepted. Then a new waiting game began. Ms. Feldman decided the book should have black and white illustrations. The editor chose illustrator Trina Schart Hyman to illustrate *A Hidden Magic*. Vande Velde was seriously impressed![12] Trina Schart Hyman had won a Caldecott Medal for the book *Saint George and the Dragon* by Margaret Hodges. The Caldecott Medal, named in honor of nineteenth-century English illustrator Randolph Caldecott, is awarded each year to the artist of the most distinguished American picture book for children. To have her first book illustrated by a Caldecott-winning artist thrilled Vande Velde.[13]

Ms. Hyman's Caldecott medal meant that the artist was booked up with illustrating work for

Vivian Vande Velde proudly holds up a copy of her first novel, *A Hidden Magic*.

many months to come. She agreed to illustrate the book, but Vande Velde and Ms. Feldman would have to wait for Ms. Hyman to complete other work on her schedule first. That wait stretched into two years.

"It had taken me two years to write the book, and two more years to send it out to thirty-three publishers," Vande Velde remembers, "and now I had to wait two more years for Trina to illustrate *A Hidden Magic!*"[14] The book, the first of many to come, was published in 1985. In the meantime, Vande Velde sold several more short pieces of her writing including "April Fool," "Of Talents and Gifts," "A Christmas Gift for the Family," and "The Great Detective of Marshall Street."[15]

While *A Hidden Magic* was the first book Vande Velde wrote, and the first to receive a contract offer, Vande Velde had finally begun writing another book. She finished it and began submitting it. Within two months of Crown's offer to purchase *A Hidden Magic*, Vande Velde received an acceptance on the second book, called *Once Upon a Test: Three Light Tales of Love*.[16] This book was also for children. It was three stories, all different perspectives on the pronouncement made by kings in so many fairy tales: "Whoever performs this feat will receive my daughter and my kingdom."

Vande Velde heard from Thea Feldman at Crown about *A Hidden Magic* in November of 1983. In January of 1984, she heard from an editor at Albert Whitman Publishers about *Once Upon a Test: Three Light Tales of Love*. Like *A*

Hidden Magic, this book would also have black and white illustrations, drawn by Diane Dawson Hearn.

This was an exciting and inspiring time for Vande Velde. She had received two acceptances on two books within two months. *Once Upon a Test: Three Light Tales of Love*, the second book Vande Velde wrote, debuted in 1984. *A Hidden Magic*, the first manuscript Vande Velde penned—her "major project" begun in the "Writing for Publication" class—hit the bookshelves in 1985.

Chapter 7

Writing for Jane

With two books accepted—one about to arrive in bookstores and libraries, and one in the publishing pipeline—Vande Velde remembers thinking, "I had better start another book!"[1] She had been spending her time writing short stories and knew that she needed to concentrate now on another novel.

By this time, Vande Velde's daughter, Elizabeth, was attending elementary school, so Vande Velde was free to work during the hours that Elizabeth was at school. It seemed like a simple enough plan to decide on some hours in which to write and then do it. But Vande Velde admits that she was not very disciplined. She never said, "Oh, I'll write for two hours a day," because there were so many fun distractions—reading, movies, lunches with friends, crocheting and the like.[2]

What Vande Velde soon learned, though, is that if she found time to write a little bit each day, the process was actually easier. A nice benefit to this kind of daily discipline was the blossoming of new ideas. "I discovered that if I wrote every day, I had more ideas—better ideas, even—and that the writing flowed more smoothly."[3]

Sometimes, Vande Velde applied her writing skills to projects for her daughter, Elizabeth. When Elizabeth was in elementary school, Vande Velde wrote a play called *The 21 Sillies* for her daughter's Girl Scout troop. "It was a compilation of small skits, where all twenty-one of us in the troop had parts," Elizabeth says. "We acted it out and earned a theatre badge for it."[4]

Vande Velde was a mother to a young child and a homemaker. She volunteered at her daughter's school. And she just happened to have book contracts! It was an exciting time for the new author.

Vande Velde was fortunate in that she did not have to do a lot of revisions on either *A Hidden Magic* or *Once Upon a Test: Three Light Tales of Love*.[5] It was somewhat of a waiting game for Vande Velde as she anticipated the publication dates of her first two books.

About the time that *A Hidden Magic* was due to come out, Vande Velde's editor on the book, Thea Feldman, called. Ms. Feldman told Vande Velde that she was leaving Crown Publishers to take a position at Golden Books. Ms. Feldman informed

Elizabeth with her Girl Scout Troop in 1989. Vande Velde wrote a play for Elizabeth's troop called *The 21 Sillies*. Elizabeth is second from the left.

Vande Velde that she would be getting a new editor at Crown. Vande Velde was at the printing stage with *A Hidden Magic*, so she was relieved that she would not have to worry about a new editor wanting major changes on the book.

A new editor meant introducing her work to someone that did not yet love it as Ms. Feldman had, however. "I was being introduced to a new editor who wanted to see something new," Vande Velde says. "And I knew I needed to write something."[6]

Vande Velde's new project was *A Well-Timed Enchantment*. Her new editor at Crown, Andrea Cascardi, accepted the book. It told the story of an American girl visiting France, but not just contemporary France—the France of 1066!

Five years elapsed between the publication of *A Hidden Magic* and *A Well-Timed Enchantment*. Vande Velde was not worrying too much, though. "I was working on writing what was to be *The Book of Mordred* and another book called *The Conjurer Princess*," she says. "I wasn't paying attention at all to the passing of time."[7]

The only time Vande Velde recalls worrying over whether she would publish another book was at book signings and book festivals. "I would go to signings, and I would only have two books, while other authors would have stacks of books," she says with a laugh.[8]

Ms. Cascardi rejected Vande Velde's next submission, a novel entitled *User Unfriendly*. *User Unfriendly* is the story of Arvin Rizalli, six friends, and his mom, who pirate a computer-generated, interactive video game that plugs right into the players' brains! Ms. Cascardi did not like the book at all, Vande Velde remembers.[9] Vande Velde felt that Crown Publishers was moving away from publishing older middle-grade novels.[10] She wondered what to do next in her writing career.

A copy of the *Bulletin*, the monthly publication of the Society of Children's Book Writers and Illustrators (SCBWI), provided an answer. Vande Velde read in the *Bulletin* that author Jane Yolen was starting an imprint at Harcourt Publishers. The imprint was to be called Jane Yolen Books.[11]

Jane Yolen is a children's writer with an impressive list of book credits of her own. She had worked as an associate editor at another publishing house, Knopf, in the Children's Book Department, in the 1960s. Yolen had been retired from editing for some years while living out in the country and raising her three children. In the late 1980s, Ruben Pfeffer and Willa Perlman, who ran the children's trade department at Harcourt, asked Yolen to edit a line of books for them.[12]

Vande Velde quickly wrote a letter to Jane Yolen about her manuscript, *User Unfriendly*. "I already knew Vivian's first book, *A Hidden Magic*, which I thought charming if a bit lightweight," Yolen says. "When Vivian sent me *User Unfriendly*, I sat down and read it in one gulp."[13]

Jane Yolen expressed an interest in purchasing *User Unfriendly*. She did not, however, offer an immediate contract. Vande Velde spent time editing and revising the book without a contract. The result was a longer book. Ms. Yolen wrote to Vande Velde and indicated that now, the story was too long. She wanted Vande Velde to cut ten thousand words from the manuscript.[14]

Yolen had been president of Science Fiction and Fantasy Writers of America (SFWA) for two years. The line of books she was acquiring and editing for Harcourt were mostly young adult fantasy and science fiction. "Vivian's book was right on the cusp of both genres," Yolen says. "I loved it, but in those pre-*Harry Potter* days, big fat novels were frowned upon."[15]

"I wasn't sure if I could cut that many words from *User Unfriendly*," Vande Velde says. "But if I didn't, I'd have to give up or submit something else for Jane to look at."[16] Vande Velde returned to her desk and proceeded to cut ten thousand words. Ms. Yolen read the resulting draft of *User Unfriendly* and offered Vande Velde a contract. The book came out in 1991.

From 1991 to 1996, Vande Velde wrote four more books under the Jane Yolen Books imprint at Harcourt: *Dragon's Bait, Tales From the Brothers Grimm and the Sisters Weird, Companions of the Night*, and *Curses, Inc.* Yolen did not accept every manuscript that Vande Velde sent to her. "I turned down *The Conjurer Princess* not once but twice because I couldn't see it as a young adult book, no matter how much I adored it," Yolen says.[17] She also never bought *A Coming Evil*, saying, "Oddly, it didn't work for me."[18]

Yolen never knew what Vande Velde was working on at any one time. "Suddenly a new book would be delivered by mail and land on my desk. I read it and usually bought it almost immediately," Yolen recalls.[19] "Her manuscripts were always different—always a surprise," Yolen says.[20] Although she remembers Vande Velde's manuscripts as tightly written, Yolen did assist Vande Velde with some line editing and some literary analysis; not much, however, she insists. Yolen saw herself more as Vande Velde's cheerleader.[21]

"My truest memory of Vivian as a writer is that she listened to everything an editor said in a revision letter, and then did what was right for the book, whether the editor had noticed a problem or not," Yolen says. Yolen remembers Vande Velde as one of the fastest writers during the revisions process that she ever worked with—including herself![22]

Yolen calls Vande Velde's *Companions of the Night* her favorite of the five books she worked on with Vande Velde. She says that in that book, Vande Velde takes an evil character and makes us understand him.[23] "She invented Buffy's 'Angel' before Angel was a character on TV," Yolen says, comparing Ethan in *Companions of the Night* with Angel in *Buffy the Vampire Slayer*.[24]

Companions of the Night was, later, one of Vande Velde's daughter's favorite books. "I remember really enjoying that book," Elizabeth says of *Companions of the Night*. "There is a small kissing scene with Kerry and Ethan, the vampire.

I was a little embarrassed while reading it—after remembering that my mom had written it! I was also a little shocked that my mother would think of those things!"[25]

Yolen's other favorite Vande Velde book is *Dragon's Bait*, a book about a girl named Alys who has been falsely accused of being a witch and condemned to be sacrificed to a dragon. A dragon named Selendrile—who is able to assume the form of a human—offers to help her get even. "I fell in love with the dragon and wanted more than anything to find a dragon like that for myself!" Yolen says.[26]

Yolen describes Vande Velde's writing style as "easy, flowing, and with a sense of humor that never stops—even in scary books!"[27] Yolen calls Vande Velde a grand writer, though vastly underrated.[28] When asked to explain, Yolen says, "Vivian has won a slew of awards, and even an Edgar from the Mystery Writers of America, but she writes rings around many of the Newbery authors."[29]

Yolen, an author herself with over sixty books to her name, describes Vande Velde as having "honed the art of storytelling to a fine and delicious edge."[30] While recognizing that Vande Velde works extremely hard at her craft, Yolen commends Vande Velde's obvious enjoyment of the process.[31] That enjoyment translates to a writing style that appears effortless. "Vivian never seems to have a lack of imagination," Yolen says.[32]

Chapter 8

Running With Ideas

There was a satisfying pattern to Vande Velde's life now. She was producing new manuscripts at a fast rate. Her books were coming out year after year. Her family life was happy and satisfying.

In 1997, Vande Velde's daughter, Elizabeth, graduated from high school. Vande Velde found she had more time than ever for her writing career. Her new freedom from the responsibilities of raising her child allowed her to begin traveling, visiting schools, and meeting her audience. Vande Velde told her editors that she was now willing to travel outside of the Rochester area and visit schools in an expanded way.[1] That visibility only added to the success of her books.

Vande Velde was not working on her writing alone. She had joined the Rochester Area

Children's Writers and Illustrators, a community of writers in her area and a network of the Society of Children's Writers & Illustrators (SCBWI). There she met writer and illustrator Mary Jane Auch. Auch was not yet published, but she attended events in the area where there were children's writers on the program. Soon, Auch joined a critique group. Critique groups are groups of writers who meet regularly to read their works and gather feedback from one another. Vande Velde was already a member of the critique group that Auch joined.[2]

"The members in our critique group have come and gone over the years," Auch says, "but Vivian and I are both still in it."[3] Vande Velde and Auch soon formed another critique group. That group consisted of eight writers who had come together after a mutual friend of theirs, Francis Temple, died. Francis's husband, Charlie Temple, taught at a nearby college and had asked the group to come in and speak to his classes. Temple talked to the writers about how much he missed being part of a critique group. "We started the group for him, but he's no longer with us," Auch says.[4] In the group, in addition to Vande Velde and Mary Jane Auch, are writers Bruce Coville, Patience Brewster, Tedd Arnold, Ellen Stoll Walsh, Cynthia DeFelice, Katherine Coville, and Robin Pulver.

Vande Velde proved herself to be excellent at the task of critiquing. "Vivian always mentions the good things about our writing," Auch explains, "but she is an expert at zeroing in on important

Vivian Vande Velde's critique group: Tedd Arnold (standing in the back) and from left to right, Mary Jane Auch, Ellen Stoll Walsh, Robin Pulver, Cynthia DeFelice, Bruce Coville, Katherine Coville, Patience Brewster, and Vivian Vande Velde.

points and telling you what isn't working in your story."[5] Auch and the other critique group members find this to be a valuable skill.

"Vivian is a superb critique-mate," says author Bruce Coville.[6] Coville praises Vande Velde's sense of structure, and her way of seeing a piece of writing at both the macro and micro levels. "She can pick upon the wrong word, and she can also tell you where the structure of a story is going awry," Coville says.[7]

Both Auch and Coville praise Vande Velde's generosity as a critique group member. "She read my book, *Song of the Wanderer*, in its entirety, and gave it a wonderful, detailed critique. That was above and beyond the call of duty," Coville says.[8]

Auch talks about hearing Vande Velde read a story once during their critique meeting. Vande Velde had sold the story as a short story to a market outside the United States, but she thought it might also work as a picture book. She had tried to market it that way but with no luck.[9]

"I heard her read that story—'Troll Teacher'— and I laughed so hard!" Auch recalls.[10] Auch told her friend Vande Velde that she thought the story would make a great picture book, too. She offered to illustrate "Troll Teacher." "I sent the story to my editor at Holiday House, and the book became *Troll Teacher*, Auch says."[11]

Vande Velde had described the troll in *Troll Teacher* as a troll with extremely hairy arms and legs. Auch recalls that while she was working on the illustrations for the book, Vande Velde would often call her. "She would ask me what I was working on, and I'd say, 'Oh, I'm painting hairs.' There were a lot of hairs," Auch explains.[12]

Auch says that the process of working with Vande Velde was a joy. "If Vivian comes up with another picture book idea, I'd be glad to collaborate with her again," she says.[13] Although she knows that most people think of Vande Velde as a writer for older kids, Auch says that Vande Velde can write for any age group.[14] Vande Velde is modest about her seemingly endless well of book ideas, but Auch is not. "Whenever we have a critique group meeting, Vivian always has something to read."[15]

In recent years, Vande Velde's books have garnered major literary awards. Her first significant award was the Nevada State Reading Award, in 1998, for her book *Companions of the Night.*

In 2000, Vande Velde's novel *Never Trust a Dead Man* was nominated for an Edgar Award. The "Edgar" is short for The Edgar Allan Poe Award, named after the Mystery Writers of America's (MWA) patron saint, Edgar Allan Poe. The Edgars are awarded to authors of distinguished work in various categories of the genre.

In *Never Trust a Dead Man*, the main character, Selwyn, is sentenced to be buried alive in a cave alongside Farold, the boy he supposedly killed. Selwyn joins forces with Farold's ghost to clear his name of Farold's murder. Vande Velde's initial idea came from watching the Orson Welles version of Shakespeare's *Othello* on TV, specifically

The Mystery Writers of America awarded Vande Velde the Edgar Allan Poe Award for her book *Never Trust a Dead Man*.

the scene in which a dead Othello and the very much alive villainous Iago are being carried away for Othello's burial. "As I watched, I thought the guards' intent was to throw Iago on the grave with Othello, and I thought, 'Yuck!' But I also thought, 'Cool!' It turned out that wasn't what the men planned . . . but that image stayed with me: the murderer and the victim buried together," Vande Velde says.[16]

"The Edgar Awards are run sort of like the Academy Awards," Vande Velde says. "There are lots of categories, and for each one, there are five nominees. So I knew in advance that I'd been nominated."[17] Vande Velde took the train to New York City. She joined her editor for *Never Trust a Dead Man*, Michael Stearns, and they sat together at the banquet. Vande Velde remembers thinking that there was no chance that she might have won the coveted Edgar in her category. Other nominees for Best Young Adult Novel included Walter Dean Myers for *Monster* and Laurie Halse Anderson for *Speak*.

The presenter for Vande Velde's category was the prolific and popular writer of children's horror stories, R.L. Stine. Before the announcement of the winners, Stine went around the room and talked to everyone in his category. "He wanted to make sure that he could pronounce everyone's name," Vande Velde says, "which I thought was so smart of him."[18]

Vande Velde recalls that the table that she sat at was the farthest one from the stage. "I didn't think that was too good a sign," she says.[19] There were many "big names" in the audience—and even some famous TV stars whose shows had been nominated for awards. Vande Velde felt certain she would not need a speech since she fully believed she would not win.

"When R.L. Stine called my name, it was a long walk to that podium," Vande Velde says. "And as I began to speak, my voice got smaller and smaller. I think that was the shortest speech of the evening!"[20] When Vande Velde received her award, she was amused to discover that the big head of Edgar Allen Poe did not even come in a box. She wrapped it in her fancy awards dress to take back to Rochester.[21]

Vande Velde's friends tease her about her Edgar. "It looks like something you'd win at a carnival," Auch says with a laugh. "But Vivian is always a good sport."[22]

"Vivian is such a generous writer and friend," Auch shares.[23] "When Vivian won the Edgar, the awards ceremony took place the day before the ceremony for the Knickerbocker Award for Juvenile Literature (given by the New York Library Association). Vivian returned from her Edgar Award ceremony in time to make it to my event and watch me receive the Knickerbocker," Auch says.[24]

Many of Vande Velde's books draw their inspiration from her personal life. *Now You See It . . .* is a good example.

At the time that Vande Velde's mother died in

Vivian Vande Velde's mother, Marcelle, in the blue and white striped dress.

2000, she did not have Alzheimer's disease, but Vande Velde remembers that her mother, Marcelle, was confused at times. Vande Velde began looking through old photo albums with her mother before she died. As Vande Velde describes it, there was a distance between her own perceptions of the old photos she looked at and the way that her mother was viewing the photographs. Vande Velde called it a "Mom Filter," a phrase she uses to describe how she only viewed her mother, before her death, as a mother.[25]

The "Mom Filter" disappeared for Vande Velde when Marcelle passed away. Vande Velde looked at the old photographs and saw her mother in a new light—as a new person and not just her mother. In one photograph, Marcelle is wearing a dress. The dress must have been special to her, Vande Velde recalls, because Marcelle kept the dress for fifty years.[26]

After Marcelle died, Vande Velde's daughter, Elizabeth, put on the blue and white striped dress. Vande Velde saw a vivid similarity between her mother and her daughter. That similarity solidified an idea that Vande Velde wanted to write about, and Vande Velde began a new book.[27]

"I suddenly saw my mother as a unique, vibrant individual," Vande Velde explains, "a woman who had a life before she became Mrs. Pat Brucato and the mother of Allan and Vivian Brucato."[28] Vande Velde wished that she had known her mother as a young woman.

That wish led Vande Velde to introduce the

Vivian Vande Velde's daughter, Elizabeth, in the same dress sixty years later. Vande Velde recounts how seeing her daughter in her mother's dress inspired her to write her character Wendy in *Now You See It* . . .

main character of *Now You See It . . .*, a girl named Wendy, who must wear glasses. After breaking her own glasses, Wendy is forced to wear a pair of mysterious glasses she finds on her lawn—sunglasses in a city that rarely sees bright sunlight. When Wendy puts the strange sunglasses on, she begins to see such things as talking dead people and blue spreenies (tiny, blue flying creatures that resemble people). One blue spreenie, Larry, joins Wendy on her jaunt back to the past. In the case of her friends Tiffanie and Julian, Wendy is able to see beyond their high-school personas to who they really are—identities that have nothing to do with Wendy's world!

In *Now You See It . . .*, Vande Velde gave Wendy a chance to meet her grandmother, Nana, as the unique, vibrant young teenager she had been long before she was Wendy's old, forgetful Nana:

> I had my head in my hands again, so all I could see was the bottom part of my rescuer's leg, with her dress billowing around her feet. She was wearing high heels. I was thinking about telling her that she shouldn't be sitting on the concrete step in her good clothes when finally I recognized the blue and white striped dress—one of a kind, handmade in Italy. Finally, I took a good look at her face.
> And *finally* I recognized that, too.
> Despite the wrong name, Eleni was my grandmother.[29]

Vande Velde wrote Nana into Wendy's story in a way that depicted Vande Velde's own longing to have known her mother, Marcelle, before she was simply "Mom."[30]

"Vivian is not only one of the best writers in the Rochester area, I think she's one of the best writers out there authoring books for kids," Auch says.[31] One of the special aspects of Vande Velde's writing, as described by Auch and the other members of Vande Velde's critique group, is the "Vivian Twist."[32] "The 'Vivian Twist' is our way of describing how the reader has no idea what is really happening in the story until the very last minute," Auch says.[33] There is always some little something at the end of Vande Velde's stories that changes everything. "Now, when we listen to Vivian read, we're looking for the 'Vivian Twist,'" Auch shares.[34]

"Vivian has an original turn of mind, and a wicked sense of humor, too," says Coville. "There's a bouncy voice that carries you along in the story—then whack! I never relax when listening to a story by Vivian, because I know at some point, she's going to hit you right between the eyes!"[35]

Coville sums up the fun of knowing Vande Velde—and reading her work—like this: "As a person, Vivian seems so nice—so normal and warm and jolly. Then there are her stories . . ."[36]

Chapter 9

School Visits, Banned Books, and No Grand Scheme

Vivian Vande Velde's thirty-first book was published in 2008, and her life continues to be about writing, selling her books, and traveling to visit children in schools. Since that first course, "Writing for Publication," that Vande Velde's husband, Jim, encouraged her to take,[1] she has grown into a phenomenon among young adult writers.

Jim is a little surprised by the success his wife has had in her writing career but not, he says, because of her talent. "Knowing how competitive the writing business is," Jim says, "I wasn't sure Vivian would excel because she isn't a competitive person by nature."[2]

Jim was not sure that Vande Velde's manuscripts would get the attention they deserved with all the many, many manuscripts vying for publication.[3] "I guess this is a testament to her talent and to her belief in herself and her work," Jim says.[4]

Vande Velde's thirtieth book, *Remembering Raquel*, is similar to her book, *Alison, Who Went Away*, in that it has no science fiction or fantasy elements. Both books grew out of Vande Velde's pondering of a couple of criminal cases in Rochester that looked as if they might never be solved. She thought about how, on TV, crimes are discovered, solved, and decided in court within an hour—so much different than in real life. "Yet there are murders for which no one is ever convicted, missing people who are never found," Vande Velde says. "What is it like, I wondered, for people who live through something like that happening in their family and they never have any closure—for those who may suspect what happened, but never know for sure?"[5]

Alison, Who Went Away is based loosely on a girl who went missing and was found dead two years later. The man who killed the girl confessed. In *Alison, Who Went Away*, the family who does not know the fate of their daughter and sister waits to learn something—but refuses to admit that Alison might be dead.

In *Remembering Raquel*, Vande Velde started with the idea of the roadside shrines that often pop up along highways after a person has died in an accident. "I wanted to write about a girl who dies and have her be remembered by various people in her life—her classmates, her teachers, a witness to the accident, the person that hit her, and even the custodian of her school!"[6] Vande Velde says. Vande Velde worked from the idea that everyone has his or her own stories—and we can only know Raquel by the combination of all her stories.[7]

Stolen is Vande Velde's thirty-first published book. In it, Vande Velde again explores the mystery of what constitutes identity. The villagers of Thornstowe finally turn on a witch with a reputation for stealing children. That same day, a twelve-year-old girl appears in the woods with no memory of her past. Is there a connection between this girl and the girl stolen by the witch six years earlier? A shocking revelation at the end of the book resolves the mystery of the girl's identity.

Vande Velde has taken on a new passion, too— fighting the censorship and banning of books. She finds that her books are now facing challenges and, in some cases, her books are being banned in certain schools. "The first time I became aware that someone could object to my books because of the fantasy element was with *User Unfriendly*, which came out in the late 1980s," Vande Velde shares.[8] A reviewer had called the book exciting and pointed out all the opportunities for discussion the book provided. "Then the reviewer said she could not recommend the book for the school because some of the parents would have a problem with the fantasy elements. I felt like a bride that has been jilted at the altar," Vande Velde says.[9]

Book banning and censorship is not new, but it has changed over time. Nowadays, more people question the reasons why some people would refuse to allow certain books into children's hands. "This is an interesting phenomenon since the J.K. Rowling *Harry Potter* books," she says. "So many people are reading the *Harry Potter* books, and I've heard of people banning the series, burning the books and other things! This has really raised visibility about banned books and the issue of censorship."[10]

In the past, people assumed that the content of a book was at fault. But with so many people reading and enjoying the *Harry Potter* books, there is an attitude of "What's the big deal?" Vande Velde thinks that it is a double-edged sword—more books are being banned, but more people are questioning why books are being banned.[11]

"It's no surprise to learn that many people think that books that have been banned or challenged must be somehow dangerous and that kids need to be protected from them. They don't realize that anyone can challenge a book," Vande Velde says.[12]

The *Harry Potter* books, because they have been read by millions of people, have allowed people to see that even though the books are fantastical and involve wizardry, "they do not promote hate or Satanism or violence. People can see that here are some perfectly innocent stories that are riling the anti-fantasy groups, and people are saying to themselves, 'What's the big deal against this book?'"[13]

Vande Velde finds it fascinating that people will ban books based on a set of titles or the genre. She writes about ghosts, yes, and magic, wizardry, and fantasy, but, she says, "I don't believe in ghosts." Vande Velde does not believe in murder, either, but her book, *Never Trust a Dead Man*, has been banned in a few places because of protesters who proclaimed, "Oh, we don't believe in murder!"[14]

Certain schools will not invite Vande Velde to visit with students because they worry that parents will have concerns about her books. "Some parents think I write dark and dangerous books," she says with a laugh.[15] Her critique group friend, Mary Jane Auch, finds this laughable, too.[16] She talks of how parents will see one of Vande Velde's books, such as *Companions of the Night*, and those parents may not want Vande Velde to visit their children's school. "But when a group of us are on a road trip, the one person that gets up and goes to church is Vivian," Auch says.[17] "She is the most ethical—the nicest—person we know."[18]

Vande Velde's book, *Alison, Who Went Away*, is not a fantasy. But the book has incited protests based on objections to the fact that the father in the book announces he is gay. People have protested Vande Velde's "gay agenda," but the girl's father is only a small part of the book. Vande Velde says that the book, unlike most of her titles, is hard to categorize, but the supposed "gay agenda" is the reason for the protests.[19]

Vande Velde's husband calls *Alison, Who Went Away* his favorite of all of Vande Velde's many books. "I believe it is her best work and remember thinking what a genius she was after reading it," he says.[20]

Another book of Vande Velde's that has been banned is *Curses, Inc.* "I only discovered that a school district in Texas had banned the book because I Googled myself," Vande Velde says.[21]

Vande Velde says that one of the worst things a parent can do is to make certain topics, issues, or books unmentionable or unattainable to his or her children. "Talk about making something irresistible," she says.[22]

As her thirty-first book is about to hit the bookstores, Vande Velde continues to write but with "no grand scheme." She says, "I just keep writing. I don't know from one book to the next what my future will bring, but I'm always grateful when I get another idea."[23] Vande Velde is modest about the numbers of published books she has out there. "I don't get that many ideas," she says, "so when I get one, I hold on to it and run with it."[24]

As far as writing styles, Vande Velde describes herself as a "plunger," meaning that she starts a story knowing only minimal details about her characters or her plot.[25] For example, in her book, *Now You See It . . .*, Vande Velde says, "I started the story knowing that somehow or other Wendy would meet her grandmother-as-a-teen and come to appreciate her, but I had no idea how or what adventures they would have together."[26]

Vande Velde shares that she generally only works on one big project at a time, although she will stop work on a novel to write a short story.[27] She does not follow any set schedule or ritual with her writing, calling herself "pretty undisciplined," and saying that she gets "distracted easily."[28]

She is quite private about her work, sharing only with her critique group members. "Vivian didn't and still doesn't share her writing with me until after publication," Vande Velde's husband, Jim, says.[29] He says that Vande Velde still has doubts after she has submitted each new manuscript. After any acceptance, Jim says, "Vivian has a period when she is sure there will never be another idea worth writing about. Then behold, another book is finished. I guess with thirty books published, she shouldn't worry about the ideas drying up, but try to convince *her* of that!"[30]

Among all her novels is her one picture book, *Troll Teacher*. "I enjoyed that experience," Vande Velde says, "and I think I may write more picture books, as well as more novels, and more themed short-story collections."[31]

Vande Velde's husband calls her an extremely talented and accomplished writer who was destined to be published.[32] Her legions of fans surely agree, as Vande Velde's books remain in print year after year.

Vande Velde says that it would be fun to be involved with movies of her books, too. "If Steven Spielberg should read one of my books," she says, "tell him to call me!"[33]

Vivian Vande Velde in May 2007.

At this point in her life, Vande Velde is enjoying writing and selling her books and traveling to schools around the country to meet her readers. When she is not actively working on her next novel, she says she "misspends" her time playing computer games. "Also, I knit, crochet, do needlepoint. Reading *does* exert a very strong pull on me. I love to be lured into someone else's world," she says.[34]

Writing for children and teenagers is Vande Velde's passion. She says:

> Writing for young people is the most important writing there is. An adult—the kind of adult who reads—is going to read hundreds of books over the 50 or 60 years of his or her (average) adulthood. Naturally, childhood is much shorter, meaning that there are only a relatively small number of books a child can read . . . it is a very short window of opportunity. And yet that is precisely the time of life when tastes and opinions are being formed—including, even, whether reading is worthwhile and if that child is going to grow up to be one of those adults who reads.[35]

"I'm not a person who plans in advance with a grand scheme," she says.[36] So far, as a writer, having no grand scheme has worked for Vivian Vande Velde.

In Her Own Words

The following interview with Vivian Vande Velde was conducted by the author via e-mail in May 2007.

How do you observe the world and find the inspiration to create your characters?

Beats me. It's a surprise every time.

I do have to say that *thinking* about a character is totally different from *writing* about that character. I can have vague ideas (someone who is spunky and feisty versus a person who is going to be trying her hardest not to get involved), but it isn't until I go from planning to actually writing that the character really takes shape—and most specifically, once my character starts talking.

Now, in some cases I've written stories in first person, and for those characters their voice is coming through from the first words of the story, because they're narrating. For example, in *Now You See It . . .*, Wendy opens her story with a rant against having to wear glasses, and the unfairness of eye doctors and eye drops. In my planning stage, I was thinking: 'Wendy wears glasses.'

In stories told in third person—or for the other characters besides the main character in a first person story—it's once the character starts talking that we truly get to know him or her. For example, in the story "As Good as Gold" in *The Rumpelstiltskin Problem*, Carleen the miller's daughter is saying things like "Yoo-hoo! Your Highness!" and "Well, *duh*." And we can immediately see what she's like much more clearly than when I thought: "She's going to be pushy." I could always have gone back and changed the words to give a different first impression. But if I think it's working, then everything gets built on that foundation.

Do you apply different skills to the different genres in which you write?

Sometimes I write for younger readers and sometimes for older, with some of my projects being short stories while others are novels.

I know going in which it's going to be.

When I wanted to write a novel about a vampire, I was aware that there are vampire novels for middle-grade students (kids 8–12). But that wasn't the kind of vampire novel I wanted to write. I wanted something for teens because I wanted *Companions of the Night* to be sensual, with the main character highly tempted by the attractive and sometimes-charming/always-dangerous vampire.

Short stories are for ideas that are much less complex—fewer characters, fewer (if any) subplots. In "To Converse With the Dumb Beasts," in *Curses, Inc.*, Kedric gets his wish, to be able to understand the speech of animals, and he finds that—in truth—they really don't have much interesting to say. That's amusing (or at least I hope it is) for nine pages. While it could be *part* of a longer story, I couldn't just have him keep running into more and more boring and/or annoying animals for the two hundred or so pages of a novel.

What made you want to write books about teenagers and magic, fantasy, time travel, and the like?

I kind of fell into this by writing the sort of things I like to read. The stories I write give me the chance to explore the questions I'm interested in.

An example: I wrote *Now You See It . . .* shortly after the death of my mother. It isn't that *Now You See It . . .* is based in any way on my mother's life, nor did I model any of the characters on her. But after my mother died, I was looking through her old photo albums (which had always been around, which I had looked through many times before). But it was only after

she was gone that—when I looked at pictures of
her as a young woman—I saw her as a young
woman and not as my mom. (And this was really
reinforced when my daughter, in her mid-
twenties, put on a dress her grandmother had
worn sixty years ago when she was in her mid-
twenties.) This was such a powerful emotional
moment for me, I even had my character in the
story wearing that same dress. It's really an
insignificant part of the story—but very important
to me.) Even though intellectually I had always
known that my mother had a life before she was
my mother, it was only then that I *really* knew
it. I suddenly saw her as someone who was
brave and resourceful, someone who had
adventures, and I thought that I really would
have liked to have known her then. So I gave
Wendy, the main character in *Now You See It . . .*,
the chance to meet her grandmother when they're
both the same age.

Do you start with a plot or a character? Give an example or two from your books.

Sometimes one, sometimes the other.

Never Trust a Dead Man started with the plot. I
wanted to write a story about someone who was
accused of something he didn't do. Specifically,
Selwyn is a young man falsely convicted of
murder. (I had no idea when I started the story
who Selwyn was as a person—besides not being a
murderer.) The villagers decide to get rid of two

problems at once: they will get rid of the dead body and get rid of the presumed murderer by locking both of them up in the burial caves. Along comes Elswyth, a witch with a short temper and a tendency to smack Selwyn on the side of the head every time he asks what she considers a dumb question, and Elswyth is willing to help him out of the caves in return for several years of his service. But escape from death isn't all Selwyn wants; he wants to clear his name by finding out who is the real murderer. The first thing he asks of Elswyth is for her to bring Farold, the dead man, back to life—just long enough to tell people who *really* murdered him. But—oops!—the spell goes wrong: Farold is brought back not in his own body, but in the body of a bat. And—oops! again—Farold was stabbed in the back, so he doesn't know who really killed him. Selwyn—with Farold-the-bat tagging along and constantly criticizing and complaining about everything—has to go back to the village to investigate the murder. Selwyn's debt to Elswyth grows longer by the minute.

Do you use a story plan or outline when writing?

I don't usually have a story plan, and I never have an outline.

Tell me about your writing process.

Usually I will start with the opening situation, plunge in, and head toward the (usually) vague

Vivian Vande Velde

idea I have for the ending. Subplots develop, often as a surprise, as a result of specific, unplanned things the characters say and do.

Yes, I know I am the author. I am in control. (More or less.) But I trust my instincts. And my subconscious. Opportunities develop.

Here's an example from *Dragon's Bait*: The main character, Alys, is someone else who has been falsely accused, in this case of being a witch. Alys and her new-found dragon friend Selendrile are approaching a town, pretending to be a pair of orphan boys. This needs to be at night because— in my rules—Selendrile can take on other forms only at night, while during the day he remains a dragon. (Sort of like a vampire can only come out at night.)

Yet I knew that, in medieval times, many of the bigger towns and cities were walled and had gates that would be barred at night. So Alys and the dragon need to speak to the guards and convince those guards to let them in. I could have written:

Alys knocked on the gate and said, "Would you please let us in? My brother and I had our home destroyed by the marauding dragon, and now we're seeking refuge."

"Oh, you poor things!" the guards said. And so they opened the gate and let them in.

But that would have been boring. Stories are about people overcoming obstacles. While it would be okay to have the guards *eventually* let them in, things couldn't go too smoothly for Alys. So I wrote that the guards both look cranky and suspicious. And then—even though I am the author, and I am in control—I found myself having one of the guards ask, "How do we know you ain't that witch?" Okay, this fits in: Alys has already been accused of being a witch, so at first—paranoid thing that she is—she worries that he knows all about her. Still, stalling for time, she asks, "What witch?" The guard answers, "That old witch lives behind one of them waterfalls up to the glen." Excuse me? What old witch who lives behind the waterfall? She hasn't been mentioned before. Still the author, still in control (more or less), I had the guard explain: "Sold her soul to the devil for the witch-power. And never did use it for nothing but mischief and sorrow all her life. But now she's old and close to dying, she's looking to buy someone else's soul to take her place." Totally unplanned. But you can't drop something like that into a story and then abandon it. Once it was written, that idea about selling one's soul—and what that means—gets revisited several times, becoming one of the themes of the story.

Do you believe in writer's block? Whether yes or no, please elaborate.

Some days the words flow easily, some days they

need quite a bit of prodding, and some days they refuse to come out at all.

Some writers have difficulty finding inspiration; others have trouble facing revisions. Finding time to write, meeting deadlines, and dealing with rejection can all be hard. What has been the most difficult part of the writing and publishing process for you?

When I'm writing a story, I invest my all in that story. Any ideas I get need to relate to that story, or that idea isn't relevant. Therefore, when I get to the end, I'm drained and I don't have a file full of ideas for my next project. I have a tendency to announce: "I don't know if I'll ever have another idea. I'll probably never write again."

After all these years of hearing that, my husband has a tendency to laugh when I say it. But that's the hardest part for me. I have all the world to choose from—how can I decide what to write next?

What is your favorite part of the writing process (i.e. new idea, getting started, writing, revision, etc.)?

For me—and some other writers would find this as hard to believe as most young people do—my favorite part is doing the revisions. I already have the story written: it's clunky, it creaks, there are coincidences and holes in the plot, too much explanation in some parts, not enough in others, missed opportunities for humor, not enough tension, pointless conversation. Now is my opportunity to polish that manuscript up and make it shine. And—for me—that's a lot easier than creating.

Heir Apparent is a slightly futuristic story about Giannine, a girl who is stuck in a computerized fantasy role-playing game. (Think one step beyond virtual reality.) She can't get out until she successfully completes the game, but—despite the risk of real brain injury if she doesn't get disconnected from the damaged, overheating equipment—she makes mistakes and keeps getting sent back to the beginning. I wanted to capture her frustration at continually having to restart—when her life is in danger, no less!—but I didn't want readers to get frustrated and feel, "This is all old information." As I was writing, I made sure that Giannine tried something new and gained useful information with each of her tries. Then, in the revision stage, I had to concentrate on making those parts that had to be repeated (waking up on the hill, meeting the other characters in the game) not sound repetitive, but different—and entertaining—at each telling.

That kind of work might sound tedious to you, but I enjoy it.

Regarding the publication of your picture book, Troll Teacher, how did it feel to have someone else illustrate your words?

Usually, an author does not get to be part of the process of choosing an illustrator or seeing sketches, so most of the covers for my novels have come as a surprise. (Usually—although I have to admit not always—a happy surprise.) I have absolutely *no* drawing talent, and so—at the very least—the cover is always better than anything I could have done. In many cases, it turns out to be better than anything I could have imagined. Since I have no drawing talent, I usually don't have a very clear picture in my head of what the characters look like. What I have is a very clear idea of their voices, and how they will speak each of their lines.

Troll Teacher was an entirely different process, because MJ (Mary Jane) Auch and I knew each other before I wrote the story. In fact, she's responsible for the book being published! She had heard me read the manuscript (which had been previously published as a short story in various newspapers and magazines), and she sent it in to her editor, who accepted the story and then asked MJ to be the illustrator. Yay!

Because I knew MJ, we discussed how the characters should look—beyond the description of the troll which I gave in the text—and I got a chance to see the pictures as they developed, which was a real treat.

I am *amazed* at MJ's talent. And grateful for her intercession with the editor. (Which is no reason for her to hint that I might occasionally hand over one or two of my royalty checks to her.)

Has any part of the book writing/book publishing process become routine for you, now that you have done it so many times?

Each book is different: new set of characters facing new situations—a new set of problems for me.

Tell me about the first award you won—what was it, for what book, and how did you feel?

One of my first short stories, "The Dragon, the Unicorn, and the Caterpillar," was published in the January 1988 issue of *Highlights for Children*, and the people at *Highlights* sent me a lovely engraved pewter plate proclaiming me "Author of the Month"—which was very sweet and exciting.

Meanwhile, my books had been honored by being on various lists put out by organizations such as the American Library Association and the International Reading Association, which is always a big deal and a happy circumstance for me.

But as far as books and awards, in 1998, *Companions of the Night* won the Nevada Young Readers' Award, in the Young Adult category. I'm not even sure if I was aware before then about state reader awards—where the young people of the state vote for their favorite book for that year. (And isn't that a great idea!) I was invited to attend the Nevada Library Association conference (clear across the country from New York State) to be introduced at the awards luncheon by a young reader and presented with the award. Very thrilling.

Some of your books have been challenged in schools. Have any been banned completely?

By Googling myself, I found out (two or three years after the fact) that *Curses, Inc.* had been officially banned—on the grounds of "Mysticism/Paganism"—from the Caldwood Elementary School Library in Beaumont, Texas. Apparently the people of Beaumont were not impressed that *Curses, Inc.* had been named an ALA Quick Pick for Reluctant Young Adult Readers, an IRA Young Adults' Choice, or a New York Public Library Book for the Teen Age.

Since I hadn't learned about this in a timely manner, it seemed too late to protest.

Have you ever been challenged about your books in person, over the phone, or via e-mail?

There have been times that I've been invited to speak at a school, then uninvited due to a single person or a small group questioning my books. On one of these occasions, the irate parent sent a letter to the editor of her local paper—which was printed, without anyone from the paper contacting me to get my side of the story. This woman's letter called my books demonic, and stated that when people read my books, the result was incidents such as the shootings at Columbine.

I tried to point out, after this letter-to-the-editor was published, that my books are fairy tales, mysteries, science fiction, and ghost stories, and that they were no more intrinsically evil than Walt Disney's *The Lion King* or the TV series *Murder, She Wrote* or *Star Trek*. I got the impression—as is often the case in such situations—that the parent was concerned enough to complain, but not concerned enough to have actually taken the time to read my books. Nonetheless, she decided my books were bad, and therefore, she equated them with other bad things. I feel that to say my books promote school shootings is just as irresponsible as to say my books cause global warming, or high gasoline prices, or juvenile diabetes.

I once had a picketer with a protest sign stand outside of a school where I was one of several speakers at a teen book fair. I am devastated that I did not get a picture of him to put up on my Website.

What is your number one bit of advice to aspiring authors?

1 If you want to write, you must read.

2 (Okay, okay, I can't follow instructions.) Don't give up.

What is next in the pipeline? What are you working on now?

Written, but so far without a home, is a novel about a girl with no memory, a witch who has a reputation for stealing children, and how the girl tries to find the connection and the missing pieces of her life.

In the process of being written is a collection of short stories all having to do with teens and psychics.

If you had not become a writer, what might your profession have been?

Before I became a writer, I was a secretary. If—thirty years later—I was still a secretary, I would have driven myself and everyone around me crazy. I can't imagine being anything besides a writer.

If I met you at a school visit or a conference, how would I know it is you?

By my big (and getting-bigger-throughout-the-day), misbehaving hair.

What is the funniest thing that has happened to you, in relation to your book-writing career?

Smart Dog won the 2002 Volunteer State (which is Tennessee) Book Award, in the Young Adult Category. Why is that funny? Because *Smart Dog* is about a fifth grade girl who meets a dog smart enough to talk, so (though I'm grateful) I don't know why it was in the "Young Adult" category. But even funnier is that—for that particular year and for the first time in Volunteer State Book Award history—there was a tie, so there were two awards given in that category. The book that got the exact same number of votes as my story about a dog smart enough to talk? *Speak*, Laurie Halse Anderson's hard-hitting novel about date rape. Not two books that have ever before (or since) been linked.

What is the funniest question you have ever been asked during a school visit?

"Do you know I have a dog?"—by a kindergarten student who had previously told me, during what was supposed to be a question and answer period, "I have a dog," only to be reminded by his teacher that he was supposed to ask a question.

Who is your favorite author?

She only wrote one book, but it's my favorite book: Harper Lee, author of *To Kill a Mockingbird*.

Who is your favorite character from your books? Why?

I can't say because then all the others would be ticked off at me.

Who are your heroes?

People who try to make the world a better place in quiet, day-to-day, non-confrontational ways. This includes those who normally get little respect from others, such as parents, teachers, doctors, hospice workers, religious people (not those who say they're religious, but those who *are*), people who are kind even when they're tired or exasperated.

If your peers were going to describe you in one word, what do you think that word would be?

Camera-nut.

I love to take pictures. I have had family and friends threaten to take my camera away from me and beat me about the head and shoulders with it.

What has been the most surprising outcome from your life as an author?

Getting fan mail. Not the kind of letters that come as part of a school project ("We have to do an Author Report, and I chose you, and if you don't write back, I won't get extra credit"), but the heartfelt letters that say "One of your books helped get me through a rough patch in my life . . ." or ". . . got me thinking about something I'd never considered before . . ." or ". . . made me like reading, when before I didn't . . ."

I knew the power of books in *my* life, but was amazed to see *my* books being so important to other people.

What is something special that you bought with one of your first writing checks?

From part of the advance for *A Hidden Magic*, we bought a grandfather clock.

How do you fill your creative well? What hobbies or activities do you enjoy when not writing?

I know it's a cliché, but what can I tell you when it's true? I love to read. It's a constant challenge to stop reading long enough to write.

Where has your favorite school visit taken you to? What trip that you have taken for leisure was your most memorable?

I enjoy school visits. Writing is solitary, and while I'm writing I can never be certain if I will ever finish the particular piece I'm working on, I don't know if I'll find an editor who wants to publish it, or if there will ever be anyone who will read it. So it's always fun to go to schools and meet some of my readers. And I have been to some extraordinary schools. But I need to tell you about two:

- Fellow Rochester writer, and teacher of at-risk high schoolers, Laurie Thurston invited me to talk to her English class, except *not* by going to their school—we had our session at Mt. Hope Cemetery. Although we had a great time—and absolutely nothing bad happened—one of the short stories in *All Hallows' Eve*, "Cemetery Field Trip," was inspired by that day.

- At East Middle School in Westminster,
  Maryland, media specialist Laurie Walters
  offered me as the prize for students who did
  best at the school's annual Read-A-Thon.
  Twelve students, one librarian, one teacher,
  and I went by limo to Medieval Times for a
  banquet and tournament. We got to eat with
  our hands and yell until we were hoarse. No
  story from that—yet. But there might be.

What is your biggest personal regret?

See the question and answer about the picketer,
the protest sign, and the missed photo
opportunity!

I have been incredibly blessed in my life. I don't
want to say that nothing has ever gone wrong,
but the things I'm grateful for far outweigh
everything else.

Did you ever in your life imagine that a biography would be written about you—and how does it feel?

I'm still not convinced that you aren't part of an
elaborate practical joke planned by [fellow
critique group members] Bruce Coville and Tedd
Arnold.

Chronology

1951— Vivian Brucato is born in New York City, New York, on June 18.

1953— The Brucato family moves to Rochester, New York.

1956— Vivian enters kindergarten at Holy Cross School already knowing how to read.

1958— Vivian begins attending Our Lady of Good Counsel School.

1965— Vivian begins high school at Nazareth Academy, an all-girls school; Vivian's father, Pat Brucato, dies; Vivian, her mother, and brother travel to Nice, France, for a two-month stay with her maternal relatives.

1969— Vivian graduates from Nazareth Academy and begins college at State University of New York (SUNY) in Brockport, New York.

1970— Vivian leaves SUNY and enrolls in a secretarial course at the Rochester Business Institute.

1971— Vivian begins working at the Rochester Telephone Company.

1973— Vivian Brucato meets Jim Vande Velde.

1974— April 20: Vivian and Jim marry.

1979— April 2: Daughter Elizabeth is born.

1981— Vande Velde finishes her first novel, *A Hidden Magic*, and begins to submit it.

1982— "Salvatore and the Leprechaun" is published in *Cricket* magazine.

1984— *Once Upon a Test: Three Light Tales of Love*, Vande Velde's second completed novel, is published by Albert Whitman Publishers.

1985— *A Hidden Magic*, Vande Velde's first completed novel, is published by Crown.

1990— *A Well-Timed Enchantment* is published by Crown.

1991— Vande Velde begins publishing under the Jane Yolen Books imprint at Harcourt Publishers with *User Unfriendly*. Vande Velde will publish five books with Jane Yolen.

1997— Vande Velde's daughter, Elizabeth, graduates from high school, and Vande Velde begins doing more traveling and school visits to promote her books.

2000—Vande Velde's mother, Marcelle Brucato, dies; Vande Velde receives the Edgar Award from the Mystery Writers of America for *Never Trust a Dead Man*; *Troll Teacher*, Vande Velde's first picture book, is published.

2001— *Alison, Who Went Away*, Vande Velde's first young adult novel without a science fiction or fantasy element, is published.

2007— Vande Velde's thirtieth book, *Remembering Raquel*, is published.

2008— Vande Velde's thirty-first book, *Stolen*, is published.

Selected Works by Vivian Vande Velde

Books

Never Trust a Dead Man

2000   *Magic Can Be Murder*

Troll Teacher

2001   *The Rumpelstiltskin Problem*

Alison, Who Went Away

Being Dead

2002   *Heir Apparent*

2003   *Wizards at Work*

Witch's Wishes

2005   *Now You See It . . .*

The Book of Mordred

Three Good Deeds

Witch Dreams

2006   *All Hallows' Eve: 13 Stories*

2007   *Remembering Raquel*

2008   *Stolen*

Additional Publications

1982   "Salvatore and the Leprechaun," *Cricket*
(reprinted in 1990 in *School Magazine: Orbit*)

1983   "April Fool," *Softalk*

"Of Talents and Gifts," *Opus Two*

1984   "A Christmas Gift for the Family," *Sunday Digest*

1985   "The Great Detective of Marshall Street,"
        Dash

1986   "The Ghost," *Upstate* (later reprinted in
        Being Dead)

        "Andrew's Baby Sister," *Living With
        Children*

        "For Love of Sunny," *Cricket* (originally
        published in *Once Upon a Test*; reprinted
        in *Girls to the Rescue*; adapted by Baker's
        Plays; reprinted in 1997 in *Storyworks*;
        reprinted in *The Best of Girls to the
        Rescue*)

1987   "Mistakes," *Buffalo Spree*

1988   "The Dragon, the Unicorn, and the
        Caterpillar," *Highlights for Children*
        (reprinted in 1994's *Valyra and the
        Dragons and Other Fanciful Adventure
        Stories* [compiled by the editors of
        Highlights for Children])

1989   "Jim-Bob and the Alien," *Aboriginal
        Science Fiction*

        "At the First Sign of Trouble," *Kid City*

        "Vampire Eyes," *Cricket* (reprinted in
        1989 in *School Magazine: Orbit*)

        "Troll Teacher," *Young American* (subse-
        quently published as a picture book;
        reprinted in 1993 in *School Magazine:
        Orbit*; reprinted in 2002 in *School
        Magazine: Blast Off*; reprinted in 2006 in
        School Magazine: Blast Off)

1990   "Suddenly," *Isaac Asimov Science Fiction Magazine*

"Recycled Grandfather," *Pulphouse: The Hardback Magazine*

1991   "Time Enough," *Amazing Stories*

1992   "Mouse," *Cricket* "A Troll Thanksgiving," *Disney Adventures* "Ebony," *School Magazine: Blast Off*

1993   "Lost Soul," *A Wizard's Dozen* (Michael Stearns: Harcourt Brace & Company; reprinted in *Curses, Inc.*)

1994   "The Beautiful Swan," *Isaac Asimov Science Fiction Magazine*

"For Love of Him," *Bruce Coville's Book of Ghosts* (Bruce Coville: Scholastic; reprinted in *Being Dead)*

"Just Another Dragon-Slaying," *Xanadu 2* (Jane Yolen: Tor; reprinted in *Spellbound)*

1995   "Tuo per sempre" ("Forever Yours"), *Nova SF* (Ugo Malaguti: Unione Stampa Periodica Italiana)

"Lian and the Unicorn," *Girls to the Rescue* (Bruce Lansky: Meadowbrook Press)

1996   "Past Sunset," *Bruce Coville's Book of Spine Tinglers* (Bruce Coville: Scholastic; reprinted in *Curses, Inc.*) *"Field Trip," Bruce Coville's Book of Aliens II* (Bruce Coville: Scholastic)

"Cypress Swamp Granny," *A Nightmare's Dozen* (Michael Stearns: Harcourt Brace & Company; reprinted in *Curses, Inc.)*

"The Granddaughter," *The Year's Best Fantasy and Horror: Ninth Annual Collection* (Ellen Datlow and Terri Windling: St. Martin's Griffin; originally published in *Tales From the Brothers Grimm and the Sisters Weird)*

1999   "A Question Concerning Witches," *Cricket*

2000   "Four Questions Concerning Witches," *Weird Tales*

2002   "The Day Rudy Saved the World," *Read*

2003   "Piper's Song," *Read*

"Dear Mr. Dickens," *Read* (reprinted in *In Short: How To Teach the Young Adult Short Story* [Suzanne I. Barchers: Heinemann])

"The Christmas Picturebook," *Democrat and Chronicle*

2004   "Morgan Roehmar's Boys," *Gothic!* (Deborah Noyes: Candlewick; reprinted in *All Hallows' Eve)*

2005   "Dear Cranky Author," *Literature for Today's Young Adults* (Kenneth L. Donelson, Alleen Pace Nilsen: Pearson Education, Inc.)

Chapter Notes

Chapter 1. Divine Intervention

1. Telephone interview with Vivian Vande Velde, December 2006.
2. Ibid.
3. Ibid.
4. Ibid.
5. Lori Atkins Goodson, "'Finish That Chapter, Then Lights Out': A Reader Becomes a Writer. A Visit With Vivian Vande Velde," *ALAN Review*, Fall 2004, p. 22.
6. Telephone interview with Vivian Vande Velde, December 2006.
7. Ibid.
8. Ibid.
9. Ibid.
10. Vivian Vande Velde, *Smart Dog* (New York: Yearling, 1998), p. 21.

Chapter 2. Clickety-Clack

1. Telephone interview with Vivian Vande Velde, December 2006.
2. Ibid.
3. Ibid.
4. Ibid.
5. Ibid.

6. Ibid.
7. Ibid.
8. Ibid.
9. Ibid.
10. Ibid.
11. Vivian Vande Velde, *Smart Dog* (New York: Yearling, 1998), p. 2.
12. Telephone interview with Vivian Vande Velde, December 2006.
13. Ibid.
14. Ibid.
15. Ibid.
16. Ibid.
17. Ibid.
18. Ibid.
19. Lori Atkins Goodson, "'Finish That Chapter, Then Lights Out': A Reader Becomes a Writer. A Visit With Vivian Vande Velde," *ALAN Review*, Fall 2004, p. 21.
20. Ibid.
21. Ibid.
22. Ibid.
23. Ibid.
24. Telephone interview with Vivian Vande Velde, December 2006.
25. Goodson, p. 21.
26. Ibid., p. 22.

Chapter 3. All Girls

1. Telephone interview with Vivian Vande Velde, December 2006.

2. Ibid.
3. Ibid.
4. Ibid.
5. Ibid.
6. Ibid.
7. Ibid.
8. Ibid.
9. Ibid.
10. Ibid.
11. Ibid.
12. Ibid.
13. Vivian Vande Velde, *A Well-Timed Enchantment* (New York: Crown Publishers, 1990), p. 2.
14. Ibid., p. 13.
15. Lori Atkins Goodson, "'Finish That Chapter, Then Lights Out': A Reader Becomes a Writer, A Visit With Vivian Vande Velde," *ALAN Review*, Fall 2004, p. 22.

Chapter 4. Speed Typing—But Not Writing

1. Telephone interview with Vivian Vande Velde, December 2006.
2. Ibid.
3. Ibid.
4. E-mail interview with Vivian Vande Velde, May 2007.
5. Ibid.
6. E-mail interview with Jim Vande Velde, May 2007.

7. E-mail interview with Vivian Vande Velde, May 2007.

8. E-mail interview with Jim Vande Velde, May 2007.

9. Ibid.

10. Telephone interview with Vivian Vande Velde, December 2006.

11. E-mail interview with Jim Vande Velde, May 2007.

12. E-mail interview with Elizabeth Vande Velde, May 2007.

Chapter 5. A Major Project of My Own

1. Telephone interview with Vivian Vande Velde, December 2006.

2. Ibid.

3. Ibid.

4. Ibid.

5. Ibid.

6. E-mail interview with Vivian Vande Velde, May 2007.

7. Telephone interview with Vivian Vande Velde, December 2006.

8. Ibid.

9. Ibid.

10. Ibid.

11. E-mail interview with Jim Vande Velde, May 2007.

12. E-mail interview with Vivian Vande Velde, May 2007.

13. Ibid.

14. Vivian Vande Velde, *A Hidden Magic* (New York: Crown Publishers, 1985), p. 1.
15. Ibid., p. 2.
16. Ibid., p. 16.
17. Karen P. Smith, "Review of *A Hidden Magic,*" *School Library Journal,* December 1985, <http://2www.amazon.com/Hidden-Magic-Vivian/dp/01520/2001> (April 4, 2008).

Chapter 6. A Hidden Magic

1. Telephone interview with Vivian Vande Velde, December 2006.
2. Ibid.
3. Ibid.
4. Ibid.
5. Ibid.
6. Ibid.
7. Ibid.
8. Ibid.
9. Ibid.
10. Ibid.
11. Ibid.
12. Ibid.
13. Ibid.
14. Ibid.
15. E-mail interview with Vivian Vande Velde, May 2007.
16. Telephone interview with Vivian Vande Velde, December 2006.

Chapter 7. Writing for Jane

1. Telephone interview with Vivian Vande Velde, December 2006.
2. Ibid.
3. Ibid.
4. E-mail interview with Elizabeth Vande Velde, May 2007.
5. Telephone interview with Vivian Vande Velde, December 2006.
6. Ibid.
7. E-mail interview with Vivian Vande Velde, May 2007.
8. Ibid.
9. Telephone interview with Vivian Vande Velde, December 2006.
10. Ibid.
11. Ibid.
12. E-mail interview with Jane Yolen, May 2007.
13. Ibid.
14. Telephone interview with Vivian Vande Velde, December 2006.
15. E-mail interview with Jane Yolen, May 2007.
16. Telephone interview with Vivian Vande Velde, December 2006.
17. E-mail interview with Jane Yolen, May 2007.
18. Ibid.
19. Ibid.
20. Ibid.
21. Ibid.
22. Ibid.
23. Ibid.

24. Ibid.
25. E-mail interview with Elizabeth Vande Velde, May 2007.
26. E-mail interview with Jane Yolen, May 2007.
27. Ibid.
28. Ibid.
29. Ibid.
30. Ibid.
31. Ibid.
32. Ibid.

Chapter 8. Running With Ideas

1. Telephone interview with Vivian Vande Velde, December 2006.
2. Telephone interview with Mary Jane Auch, May 2007.
3. Ibid.
4. Ibid.
5. Ibid.
6. Telephone interview with Bruce Coville, May 2007.
7. Ibid.
8. Ibid.
9. Telephone interview with Mary Jane Auch, May 2007.
10. Ibid.
11. Ibid.
12. Ibid.
13. Ibid.
14. Ibid.
15. Ibid.

16. Debbi Michiko Florence, "An Interview With Children's Author Vivian Vande Velde," 2004, <http://www.debbimichikoflorence. com/author_interviews/2004/VivianVande Velde.html> (April 15, 2008).

17. E-mail interview with Vivian Vande Velde, May 2007.

18. Ibid.

19. Ibid.

20. Ibid.

21. Ibid.

22. Telephone interview with Mary Jane Auch, May 2007.

23. Ibid.

24. Ibid.

25. Telephone interview with Vivian Vande Velde, December 2006.

26. Ibid.

27. Ibid.

28. Ibid.

29. Vivian Vande Velde, *Now You See It . . .* (New York: Harcourt, Inc., 2005), pp. 126–127.

30. Telephone interview with Vivian Vande Velde, December 2006.

31. Telephone interview with Mary Jane Auch, May 2007.

32. Ibid.

33. Ibid.

34. Ibid.

35. Telephone interview with Bruce Coville, May 2007.

36. Ibid.

Chapter 9. School Visits, Banned Books, and No Grand Scheme

1. E-mail interview with Jim Vande Velde, May 2007.
2. Ibid.
3. Ibid.
4. Ibid.
5. Debbi Michiko Florence, "An Interview With Children's Author Vivian Vande Velde," 2004,<http://www.debbimichikoflorence. com/author_interviews/2004/VivianVande Velde.html> (April 15, 2008).
6. E-mail interview with Vivian Vande Velde, May 2007.
7. Ibid.
8. Vivian Vande Velde, "Banned Books," last updated April 15, 2006, <http://www. vivianvandevelde.com/bannedBooks.cfm> (April 15, 2008)
9. Ibid.
10. Telephone interview with Vivian Vande Velde, December 2006.
11. Ibid.
12. Florence, "An Interview With Children's Author Vivian Vande Velde."
13. Ibid.
14. Telephone interview with Vivian Vande Velde, December 2006
15. Ibid.

16. Telephone interview with Mary Jane Auch, May 2007.
17. Ibid.
18. Ibid.
19. Telephone interview with Vivian Vande Velde, December 2006.
20. E-mail interview with Jim Vande Velde, May 2007.
21. Telephone interview with Vivian Vande Velde, December 2006.
22. Florence, "An Interview With Children's Author Vivian Vande Velde."
23. Telephone interview with Vivian Vande Velde, December 2006.
24. Ibid.
25. Debbie Michiko Florence, "Follow-up Interview With Vivian Vande Velde 2005," <http://www.debbimichikoflorence.com/author_interviews/2005/VandeVeldeUpdate05.html> (April 15, 2008).
26. Ibid.
27. Telephone interview with Vivian Vande Velde, December 2006.
28. Ibid.
29. E-mail interview with Jim Vande Velde, May 2007.
30. Ibid.
31. Telephone interview with Vivian Vande Velde, December 2006.
32. E-mail interview with Jim Vande Velde, May 2007.

33. Telephone interview with Vivian Vande Velde, December 2006.

34. Florence, "An Interview With Children's Author Vivian Vande Velde."

35. Lori Atkins Goodson, "'Finish That Chapter, Then Lights Out': A Reader Becomes a Writer. A Visit With Vivian Vande Velde," *ALAN Review*, Fall 2004, p. 22.

36. Telephone interview with Vivian Vande Velde, December 2006.

Glossary

accolades—Awards or honors signifying approval or distinction.

ambivalent—Uncertain or unable to decide what course to follow.

anachronism—Something located at a time when it could not have existed or occurred.

autobiographical—About a person's own life.

banning—An official prohibition or edict against something.

censorship—Banning or deleting objectionable parts of publications, movies, music, etc.

contemporary—Characteristic of the present or belonging to the present time.

epiphany—A clear appearance or sudden understanding.

euphemism—A word or phrase that particular people use in particular situations; sometimes an inoffensive phrase used to indicate something more offensive.

genre—A class of art or artistic endeavor such as writing having a characteristic form or technique.

G.I.—A nickname for a U.S. soldier, derived from the term *Government Issue.*

parochial—Of, relating to, supported by, or located in a parish, or local church community.

persona—A personal façade that someone presents to the world.

phenomenon—Something or someone that is impressive or extraordinary.

polarize—To divide into sharply opposing factions, political groups, etc., especially with regard to explosive issues.

posthumously—Published after the death of an author.

prerequisite—Required or necessary as a condition.

shorthand—A method of rapid handwriting using simple strokes, abbreviations, or symbols that designate letters, words, or phrases.

speed typing—The ability to type in a rapid and accurate manner.

typewriter—A writing machine that produces characters similar to typeset print by means of a manually operated keyboard that moves a set of raised types, which strike the paper through an inked ribbon; typewriters have been replaced by personal computers.

word processing—The writing, editing, and production of documents, as letters, reports, and books, through the use of a computer program or a complete computer system designed to facilitate rapid and efficient manipulation of text.

Further Reading

Hill, Christine M. *Ten Terrific Authors for Teens*. Berkeley Heights, N.J.: Enslow Publishers, Inc., 2000.

Willett, Edward. *J.R.R. Tolkien: Master of Imaginary Worlds*. Berkeley Heights, N.J.: Enslow Publishers, Inc., 2004.

Internet Addresses

Vivian Vande Velde's Web site
http://www.VivianVandeVelde.com

Interview with Vivian Vande Velde at Harcourt Books
http://www.harcourtbooks.com/authorinter views/bookinterview_velde.asp

Author Spotlight on Vivian Vande Velde at Random House Books
http://www.randomhouse.com/teens/authors/ results.pperl?authorid=31972

Index